Praise for I Won't Back Down

"Glenn masterfully guides readers on an inspiring journey of resilience and growth, weaving together compelling examples from iconic musicians with bravely candid insights from his own personal and professional experiences. His entertaining and insightful observations, combined with practical prompts, spark thought-provoking questions that empower educators to reflect, grow, and excel as both professionals and human beings.

"This book is a valuable resource for anyone. It offers a much-needed primer on building resilience, fostering innovation, and cultivating perseverance to achieve the highest levels of success for ourselves, our students, and our colleagues."

Laurence Cocco
Digital Learning Consultant and Former NJDOE Educational Technology Director

"Glenn's captivating book explores the struggles and successes of musicians alongside his own personal stories of resilience. By sharing his experiences, he allows educators to connect with him personally while his practical strategies empower educators to grow and navigate their [own] challenges. Each chapter captures attention, encourages reflection, and keeps readers engaged until the end. This book is worth reading!"

Dr. Melissa Collins
Tennessee Teacher of the Year 2022–2023

"Education can be a gut punch some days. Knowing how others have persisted in the face of outright rejection—and flourished—is just what Glenn Robbins delivers in this lively, accessible, and relatable book. If Jimi Hendrix can be booed off stage repeatedly and still become a rock legend, you can definitely overcome an awkward staff meeting or a failed back-to-school night. Glenn's book is stuffed with biographical examples of your favorite musicians persisting, thriving, and becoming legends. There are so many lessons in here for educators."

Jon Corippo
Eduprotocols Co-Creator, Educator, Author

"In *I Won't Back Down: How Educators Can Turn Rejection Into Redirection*, Glenn Robbins masterfully demonstrates how to transform the pain of rejection into a tool for resilience. Using anecdotes from the lives of famed musicians such as Elvis Presley, Tom Petty, Andrea Bocelli, and even Taylor Swift, Robbins parallels challenges in their journeys with the experiences of educators who are so frequently subjected to harsh and discouraging feedback. It's a must-read for those searching for meaning in the face of life's challenges."

Theresa Daem
Founder, National Association of School Superintendents

"*I Won't Back Down* is more than just a book—it's a conversation with a mentor who's been through the trenches and come out stronger. Glenn Robbins masterfully blends heartfelt personal stories, lessons from legendary musicians, and practical advice tailored specifically for educators navigating the challenges of rejection.

"What makes this book stand out is its unique perspective on how rejection can spark creativity and lead to growth. Glenn doesn't just offer encouragement—he provides actionable strategies to help educators transform setbacks into opportunities. Each chapter is a reminder that even in the hardest moments, there's a lesson waiting to be uncovered.

"Equally powerful is Glenn's ability to connect educators to the broader human experience. By weaving in stories of resilience from iconic musicians, he shows how struggles transcend professions and eras, leaving readers feeling inspired and connected to something bigger.

"Whether you're a leader, teacher, or just someone passionate about making a difference in education, *I Won't Back Down* will leave you feeling seen, supported, and ready to tackle whatever comes your way. This is a book I'll be revisiting often—and recommending to colleagues even more."

Amy M. Dujon
Vice President of ETC, Educational Community Author, and Speaker

"*I Won't Back Down* is a blend of practical wisdom, personal reflection, and inspiration for anyone navigating the challenges of a career in education. Glenn invites readers to join him on his journey using the lessons of music legends as parallels to his own experiences throughout his career. The stories of Bob Dylan, Johnny Cash, Taylor Swift, and the Supremes offer a unique and entertaining way to showcase how universal the struggle to be successful is. The result is a book that is highly engaging and insightful.

"It's not just a book for teachers and administrators, though; it's a roadmap for anyone looking to transform failure into success. Glenn's words are a reminder that we all have the resilience to rise, the creativity to adapt, and the power to inspire. Several times, I thought I was reading a personal message meant just for me. In a word, this book is highly relatable and relevant. Glenn Robbins has created a timeless resource that will leave readers feeling seen, heard, and ready to face the challenges ahead—with a little rock 'n' roll as their guide."

Michael Dunlea
Global Teacher Prize Top 50, Presidential Award Winner, and National Board Certified Teacher

"As educators, we are no strangers to the challenges and setbacks inherent in nurturing young minds. In *I Won't Back Down: How Educators Can Turn Rejection Into Redirection*, Glenn Robbins offers a powerful testament to the resilience required to turn rejection into a stepping stone for success.

"This book is not just a collection of inspiring stories; it is a critical roadmap for any educator navigating the complexities of professional growth and personal fulfillment. Glenn masterfully intertwines the lessons from musical legends with practical strategies for educators, reminding us that our greatest trials can lead to our most profound triumphs.

"I wholeheartedly recommend this book to anyone in the educational sector looking to transform challenges into opportunities for innovation and impact."

Dr. Zandra Jo Galvan
Superintendent of Schools, Salinas Union High School District

"*I Won't Back Down* feels like a heartfelt conversation with a friend who truly gets it. As someone who's faced rejection and been overlooked myself, I found so much hope and reassurance in Glenn's ability to reframe those tough moments into opportunities for growth.

"Through inspiring personal stories and well-framed lessons from legendary musicians, Glenn shows us how to turn setbacks into springboards. It's the perfectly uplifting professional hug you need to remind yourself of your own worth. Glenn's honest, encouraging tone and practical advice make this book a true gift for educators—or anyone—looking for a little light on the path to resilience and success."

Kathi Kersznowski
Educational Technology Specialist and Owner of
Integration Innovation, LLC

"Glenn's newest book, *I Won't Back Down: How Educators Can Turn Rejection Into Redirection*, creates a tapestry of leadership lessons taken from the soundtrack of our lives. Song lyrics provide powerful value statements that touch the hearts of individuals and connect teams across generations. Glenn's themes strike a chord for reflective educators to ground themselves and to grow their leadership through values."

Kirk Koennecke
CEO Indian Hill EVSD and 2023 NASS Superintendent of the
Year

"I recommend *I Won't Back Down: How Educators Can Turn Rejection Into Redirection* as a vital read for educational leaders and aspiring educators alike. Glenn's personal journey, infused with lessons from iconic musicians, highlights resilience, the transformative power of rejection, and the importance of mentorship. He masterfully weaves personal anecdotes with professional insights, providing actionable strategies for educators navigating challenges and seeking growth.

"This book resonates deeply, reinforcing the value of persistence, collaboration, and innovation in education. It aligns perfectly with leading with the heart, supporting educators, and embracing the challenges that mold us into impactful leaders."

Travis Lape
Director of Teaching and Learning

"Glenn Robbins masterfully bridges the gap between educational discipleship, great musicians of our time, and the power of perspective shift. As a true *pontifex maximus*, or 'bridge builder,' Glenn offers compelling narratives where he illuminates how the trials and tribulations inherent in every educator's journey can become catalysts for reinvention and redirection.

"His insightful exploration of key disruptors in education serves as a rallying cry, reminding us that backing down is not an option for those dedicated to shaping young minds and making a difference. This book stands as a testament to the transformative power of action and perseverance in the face of rejection, offering a roadmap for educators to practice redirection."

Christopher J. Nagy Ed.D., M.A., C.A.P.P.
Founder and President of Nagy Education Group

"Calling all music fans! This book is more than just a chronicle of hardships faced; it's also a celebration of unwavering courage and positive outcomes through perseverance. Glenn's journey, mirroring some of the most iconic musical greats as they hit low and high notes, is nothing short of inspiring. The stories resonate deeply and will remind you that every setback can lead to a greater comeback. A must read for anyone seeking motivation and insight!"

Aleng Phommathep
Award-Winning Chief Technology Officer

"In *I Won't Back Down*, Glenn Robbins connects stories of legendary musicians like Johnny Cash and Tom Petty to the challenges educators face every day. With practical advice and relatable examples, he inspires teachers and leaders to turn rejection into opportunities, embrace resilience, and take bold risks. This empowering guide shows how setbacks can lead to success and will leave you motivated to keep pushing forward."

Asael Ruvalcaba, M.Ed.
Educational Leader and Mentor

"Glenn Robbins masterfully reframes rejection as a catalyst for growth in his thought-provoking book. Through deeply personal stories and relatable anecdotes, he challenges educators to see setbacks not as failures but as opportunities for redirection and resilience.

"Robbins provides a roadmap for transforming moments of defeat into key turning points, equipping readers with practical strategies and an inspiring vision for their careers. This book is an empowering guide for any educator looking to harness the power of rejection to fuel their success and rediscover their purpose."

Joe Sanfelippo, Ph.D.
Retired Superintendent, Author, Speaker

"*I Won't Back Down* is a powerful and inspiring guide for educators facing rejection and seeking growth. Glenn Robbins illustrates how setbacks can become opportunities for reinvention and success. Each chapter delivers practical strategies and heartfelt encouragement, empowering educators to turn challenges into triumphs and find their authentic path. It is a must-read for anyone striving to thrive in the ever-evolving world of education."

Winston Y. Sakurai, Ed.D.
2016 NASSP National Digital Principal of the Year and 2016 HASSA Hawaii State Principal of the Year

"I have read many books while in academia, but not many have touched me like *I Won't Back Down* by Glenn Robbins. In education, there is a dark area that creates obstacles for many in their careers. Glenn does a magnificent job of connecting his struggles in becoming a district leader with those of popular artists who were not initially deemed worthy for success.

"Take a ride with Glenn on this journey that will allow you to think, reflect, and overcome. After three decades in education, I have found a book that helps me reflect on my journey as an educator. This is a must-read."

Josh Tovar
Principal and Host of #PGPPODCAST

"*I Won't Back Down* by Glenn Robbins truly connected with me as a person, leader, educator, and father. The power of resilience to get us through rejection and failure, to help us embrace all the struggles and turn them into opportunities and triumphs, is the key to growth for any individual. I truly recommend the book to every educator who wants to foster a growth mindset."

Dr. Angello Villarreal
Teacher at Freehold Township High School and National Award-Winning Educator

"*I Won't Back Down* is the formula and guidebook you need to bring yourself and your teaching to the next level. Music + personal experiences + lessons for growth = getting better! I've known Glenn for many years, and this is a must-read book that's going to help you in whatever job you currently have. Five stars! Two thumbs up!"

Adam Welcome
Educator, Author, Speaker, Podcaster

I WON'T BACK DOWN

HOW EDUCATORS CAN TURN REJECTION INTO REDIRECTION

GLENN ROBBINS

Book Cover by Michael Smith

ISBN (paperback): 979-8-218-59892-1
ISBN (ebook): 979-8-218-59893-8

For Abigail

You've given me more than anything I could dream of.

Contents

Introduction 1

1. The Power of Support 11

2. Finding the Right Fit 17

3. The Long Road to Success 25

4. Enduring Repeated Rejections 31

5. The Importance of Mentorship 37

6. Innovating and Evolving 43

7. Overcoming Hardship 49

8. The Struggle for Recognition 55

9. Taking a Different Path 61

10. Breaking Down Barriers 67

11. Challenging Expectations 73

12. The Power of Passion 79

13. Overcoming Adversity 87

14. Celebrating Differences 95

15. The Alternative Route to Success 103

Conclusion 109

I Won't Back Down Playlist 115

About the Author 117

Introduction
Embracing Rejection as Redirection

We all learn lessons in life. Some stick, some don't.
I have always learned more from rejection and
failure than from acceptance and success.

Henry Rollins

"**S**on, I suggest you go to church, light a candle, and pray someone dies or retires. That's the only way you'll get a job here."

His words, blunt and dismissive, hit like a punch to the side of the head. I had barely worked up the courage to talk to this man, and here he was crushing my spirit without a second thought.

He was the superintendent of a school district I admired, and when I saw him in the hallway, I knew I was lucky to cross his path. Despite my heart thumping in my chest, I had to seize the opportunity to introduce myself.

I had just graduated at the completion of the winter semester, and my college loan payments were already coming due. I didn't have the luxury of waiting for opportunities to come to me, so I did what I thought would give me a competitive edge—I visited 20-plus school districts, résumé and cover letter in hand, determined to make an impression. My plan was to personally hand them to the principal and superintendent in each district.

Most of my attempts were met by office staff who politely took my documents without letting me get beyond the front desk. Despite that, I remained hopeful and determined.

After that superintendent's harsh wake-up call, though, it was hard to feel anything except dismay. I remember driving home feeling utterly defeated. My mind raced with questions: Was this how the real world worked? Were opportunities in education so scarce that my only hope was dumb luck or someone else's tragedy? Self-doubt crept in, making me question whether all my efforts were futile.

It was my first taste of rejection in my journey as an educator, but it certainly wouldn't be my last.

In today's fast-paced and ever-evolving educational landscape, rejection has become an all-too-familiar experience for many. Whether it's in the form of unsuccessful job interviews, critical feedback on teaching methods, a vision that doesn't align with the institution's, or even a layoff or termination, rejection can be a deeply painful blow.

But considering all the challenges facing today's educators, why focus on rejection, and why now? Because more educators than ever are facing professional setbacks; it's not so much a result of individual failure but rather a reflection of the pressures and rapid changes in the field. I've personally witnessed how frequently rejection affects even the best educators—passionate individuals whose work is often met with shifting expectations, systemic challenges, and limited resources.

If you haven't faced much rejection in your career, you might be wondering why you should care about this issue. First of all, just because you haven't faced rejection yet doesn't mean you won't. In fact, I'd go so far as to say you *will* face it. When you do, you don't want to be blindsided by it like I was. Let this book help you prepare.

Secondly, being prepared for rejection is just the beginning. What's more important is understanding that rejection can be a powerful force for redirection. Yes, rejection can be a detour in disguise for the better.

This book explores how rejection, rather than being a mark of failure, can become a transformative experience for educators. Drawing from personal stories, historical examples, and practical strategies, I will show you how to harness the lessons embedded in rejection and use them to fuel your growth, resilience, and ultimate success.

This is a book for every educator—whether a paraprofessional, teacher, school administrator, or district administrator—who has faced (or will face) rejection, doubted their worth, or struggled to find their place. You are far from alone, and together, we can turn rejection into one of the most powerful tools for personal and professional evolution.

Rejection Is Redirection

I didn't know it at the time, but that discouraging interaction with the superintendent I admired was an important part of steering me toward the right path. Soon after, I landed an interview and eventually a job offer from a district where my persistence had actually reached the principal. The door that had been slammed in my face in one place was just a detour toward a better opportunity elsewhere.

Consider the stories of successful individuals who faced repeated rejections before achieving their dreams. Like mine, these stories are not anomalies. They exemplify a common truth: Rejection often serves as a powerful form of redirection for something so much better than ever expected.

When we experience rejection, it can be the universe's way of steering us away from paths that are not meant for us and guiding us toward opportunities that better align with our true potential and purpose.

In a 2005 commencement address at Stanford University, Steve Jobs highlighted how this played out in his own life after he got fired from Apple, a company that he co-founded:

> What had been the focus of my entire adult life was gone, and it was devastating. I really didn't know what to do for a few months . . . But something slowly began to dawn on me—I still loved what I did. The turn of events at Apple had not changed that one bit . . . I didn't see it then, but it turned out that getting fired from Apple was the best thing that could have ever happened to me. The heaviness of being successful was replaced by the lightness of being a beginner again, less sure about everything. It freed me to enter one of the most creative periods of my life.[1]

Getting fired forced Jobs to shift his mindset, viewing rejection not as a personal failure but as a necessary step toward something greater. It serves as a reminder that some of the very best and brightest the world has ever seen have been rejected and fired, only to rise back up better than before.

Rejection Can Lead to Growth

Rejection forces us to reflect on our goals, motivations, and approaches. It compels us to reevaluate and refine our strategies, often leading to breakthroughs that would not have been possible otherwise. This process of reflection and adjustment is crucial for personal and professional development.

For example, consider an educator who faces rejection when their innovative teaching proposal is turned down by the school administration. While the initial response may be disheartening, this rejection can serve as a valuable opportunity to revisit and enhance the proposal, seek feedback, and perhaps find alternative platforms to implement their ideas. Through this reflective process, the educator's work becomes stronger and more impactful.

Rejection Is a Tool for Resilience

Rejection also builds resilience. Each time we face a setback and choose to persevere, we strengthen our capacity to endure and overcome future challenges. This resilience is a crucial ingredient for success in any field.

"Resilient individuals recognize that failure is an inherent part of the learning process, and it is an opportunity to develop new skills and insights," writes Jack Kelly of *Forbes*.[2] "Instead of denying or avoiding it, you must face failure with honesty and openness." He goes on to explain that failure (or rejection) is not an indication of your value; it's a chance to grow and improve.

In fact, in many cases, growth and improvement aren't possible without the resilience that comes from rejection. It is the ability to bounce back, learn from experiences, and persist in the face of adversity that often distinguishes those who achieve their dreams from those who do not.

Your Rejection Isn't on Display

One of the most paralyzing aspects of rejection is the fear of being judged by others. We often imagine that when we fail, lose a job, or face public setbacks, everyone is watching and silently criticizing us. Yet this fear is often unfounded; most people are too preoccupied with their own lives and concerns to scrutinize ours.

Brené Brown, in her award-winning book, *Daring Greatly: How the Courage to Be Vulnerable Transforms the Way We Live, Love, Parent, and Lead*, delves into the dynamics of vulnerability and shame, noting that "vulnerability is like being naked onstage and hoping for applause rather than laughter. It's being naked when everyone else is fully clothed."[3]

Brown points out that our fear of judgment is often a projection of our own insecurities. This aligns with the "spotlight effect," a well-documented cognitive bias in which individuals tend to overestimate the degree to which others notice their mistakes or shortcomings.[4]

In essence, human beings are inherently self-focused, and the judgments we assume others hold about us often exist only in our minds. Understanding this truth is liberating: It frees us from the paralyzing fear of public opinion, empowering us to take risks, embrace setbacks, and ultimately pursue growth without the weight of imagined scrutiny.

Rejection Can Point to Your True Path

Finally, embracing rejection as a positive force can help us find our true path. When we are forced to pivot and explore new directions, we may discover passions, talents, and opportunities that we would have otherwise missed. This journey of exploration and discovery can lead us to places where we truly belong—places that resonate with our deepest values and aspirations. All of these detours are blessings in disguise.

In this book, we will delve into the stories of individuals who have turned rejection into triumph, explore the psychological and emotional aspects of facing setbacks, and provide practical strategies for using rejection as a tool for personal and professional growth. By the end, you will have a new perspective on rejection, seeing it not as an obstacle but as a powerful catalyst for a better, more fulfilling life.

So the next time you face rejection, remember: It's not the end of your journey but rather a redirection toward something even greater. Embrace it, reflect on it, and use it as a stepping stone to reach your true potential.

Learning from Musical Artists

I've always been fascinated by musicians, perhaps because music has the power to capture and express emotions that words alone sometimes cannot. One of the many powers of music is that it's as close to a time machine as we can get. When we hear certain songs, we can recall where we were, how we felt, and what event was taking place when we first heard it.

Growing up, I was part of the Columbia House music club, which would mail out 10 CDs for only a dollar. As a young kid, I would eagerly await those packages, and once they arrived, I'd listen to the songs on repeat and study the album covers with curiosity and admiration. Each artist and each album had a story to tell—many of failure and rejection that ultimately led to triumph.

Now as an adult, I still love these songs, but there's a new dimension to them. Through their stories, I've realized how similar the journey of musicians is to that of educators. Musicians live under a spotlight where their every move is scrutinized, and often, they are passed over for record deals or awards because someone doesn't believe in the song(s). Sometimes their albums flop or their work is misunderstood by critics. Yet time and again, many of these artists transform these rejections into opportunities for reinvention and growth.

In the same way, educators are often subject to insensitive feedback and harsh criticism from supervisors, colleagues, media, political leaders, parents, and even students. This can feel overwhelming and discouraging, but like musicians, educators can use rejection to refine their craft and discover new strengths.

In this book, I relate the stories of musicians because their resilience in the face of rejection is universally relatable and inspiring, especially for those of us in education. The lessons from their lives and careers are particularly relevant because, in both music and education, creativity and perseverance are key.

Whether it's a musician writing a hit song after a career setback or an educator finding a breakthrough with students after a tough review, the message is clear: Rejection doesn't define us—it redirects us. It pushes us toward something better, as long as we are willing to learn from it and keep moving forward.

I've realized that, much like the tales in the songs I poured over as a kid, every rejection story is a path toward something more authentic and meaningful. That's why the lives of musicians resonate with me—they show that the journey toward improvement is never linear but always worthwhile. I hope their stories inspire you as well.

---

1. Stanford University, "'You've Got to Find What You Love,' Jobs Says," *Stanford Report*, June 12, 2005, https://news.stanford.edu/stories/2005/06/youve-got-find-love-jobs-says/.

2. Kelly, Jack, "How to Be Resilient Amid Failure and Uncertain Times," *Forbes*, January 24, 2024, https://www.forbes.com/sites/jackkelly/2024/01/24/how-to-be-resilient-amid-failure-and-uncertain-times/.

3. Brown, Brené, 2012, *Daring Greatly: How the Courage to Be Vulnerable Transforms the Way We Live, Love, Parent, and Lead*, Avery, p. 26.

4. Raypole, Crystal, "Always Feeling Self-Conscious? Here's Why You Shouldn't According to Science," *Healthline*, July 30, 2020, https://www.healthline.com/health/mental-health/spotlight-effect/.

CHAPTER 1

The Power of Support
Tom Petty

Oh, I get by with a little help from my friends.
John Lennon and Paul McCartney

In the late 1980s, Tom Petty was already a well-established rock musician with a string of hits and a loyal fan base. However, even seasoned artists face setbacks, and for Petty, one of his most significant challenges came with the creation of his iconic album *Full Moon Fever*. Initially rejected by music executives who couldn't see its potential,[1] the album's journey to international success is a testament to resilience, the power of supportive allies, and the unpredictable nature of creative genius.

Initial Rejection

Tom Petty poured his heart and soul into *Full Moon Fever*, an album that he felt represented some of his best work. Among the standout tracks was "Free Fallin'," a song that captured the essence of Southern California and resonated deeply with Petty's personal experiences. Confident in the album's quality, Petty presented it to his record label, expecting enthusiasm and support.

To his dismay, the executives were unimpressed. They critiqued the album as lacking commercial viability, insisting no one would buy it. This rejection was a significant blow to Petty who had invested a huge amount of creative energy into the project. The dismissal sent him into a state of depression as he grappled with self-doubt and frustration.

George Harrison's Redirection

Enter George Harrison, the former Beatle and Petty's friend and collaborator. Recognizing the brilliance of *Full Moon Fever* and understanding the subjective nature of the music industry, Harrison decided to intervene. With his clout and experience, Harrison knew that sometimes it takes the right person to recognize and champion great art.

Harrison leveraged his connections and influence, championing the album to other music executives at a dinner. Later that night, he asked Petty to riff with him on the new album he was working on, and as they did, the listeners couldn't ignore Petty's talent.

Triumph and Success

Thanks to Harrison's persistent advocacy, the narrative around *Full Moon Fever* began to change. The album was eventually picked up by executives who saw its potential after learning that others wanted to sell it.

Upon its release, the album became a monumental success. "Free Fallin'" soared up the charts, becoming one of Petty's most beloved songs and an enduring classic. But "Free Fallin'" was just the beginning. The album also featured other hit tracks such as:

- "I Won't Back Down": An anthem of resilience and

determination, this song became a staple of Petty's live performances and a rallying cry for many (including me).

- "Runnin' Down a Dream": With its driving rhythm and evocative lyrics, this track celebrated the pursuit of dreams and became a rock radio favorite.

- "Yer So Bad": A quirky, catchy tune that showcased Petty's wit and storytelling prowess.

- "A Face in the Crowd": As a more introspective song, this highlighted Petty's ability to blend personal reflection with universal themes.

The album earned critical acclaim and commercial success, affirming Petty's artistic vision and resilience.

My Personal Journey

"We almost didn't hire you, but based on your previous situations, we knew you could handle all the bullshit that would be thrown at you, and we believe you can handle anything."

At first, I was taken aback by his candidness. After all, we had just met. It was only a few weeks earlier that the school board had hired me for a leadership role, and this was my first conversation with the mayor.

Aside from that, I was surprised that this was how he felt about me. My own perception was entirely different. During the hiring process, I had been focused on my struggles, failures, and shortcomings. In fact, I was kind of shocked I got the job. But what I hadn't considered was how much those setbacks had shaped me into a stronger, more resilient leader, and how that was becoming apparent to others.

That day when the mayor shared his perspective, informed by his own leadership journey, it was a gift—a reminder that my challenges don't just test me, they refine me. I still have deep appreciation for his words because they helped me realize that leadership is often about surviving the storm and emerging on the other side—not unscathed, per se, but stronger and more capable than before.

But they also helped me understand that sometimes others see our growth before we do, and they push us to keep moving forward. The conversation reminded me that in education, leadership, and life, what we perceive as delays or defeats can often be viewed as resilience and determination by those who have walked similar paths.

Lessons for Educators

The journey of *Full Moon Fever*, like my conversation with the mayor, offers valuable lessons for educators. Just as Petty faced skepticism from his record label, you may encounter leaders who fail to recognize the potential of your innovative ideas. However, rejection does not necessarily mean the end of the road. Instead, it can be an opportunity to seek out allies who understand and appreciate your vision.

Tom Petty's journey with *Full Moon Fever* underscores the importance of perseverance and the power of having a supportive network. For educators, the lesson is clear: Not every boss or leader will recognize the genius of an idea right away. However, with persistence, resilience, and the support of others, innovative ideas can find their way to success.

Here are four ways to put this lesson into action:

1. **Identify supportive allies.** Like Petty found support

in Harrison, seek out colleagues, mentors, and leaders who can champion your ideas. These allies can provide the necessary support and advocacy to push projects forward.

2. **Face rejection with resilience**. Rejection is a part of any creative and innovative process. Work on developing resilience and viewing setbacks as opportunities to refine and strengthen your ideas.

3. **Leverage your network**. Once you have a network of supportive and influential individuals, don't be afraid to use it to help you navigate the complexities of institutional approval. Just as Harrison used his connections to support Petty, leverage your network to find the right audience for your ideas or to champion the ideas of someone else.

4. **Be persistent.** Remain persistent in advocating for your ideas, even in the face of initial rejection. Often, the key to success lies in continuing to believe in your vision and seeking alternative pathways to make it a reality.

Write Your Own Lyrics

1. Identify colleagues or mentors who can act as supportive allies in championing your innovative ideas. How can you cultivate relationships with them? What can you give back in return for their support?

2. Reflect on a time when you faced rejection or skepticism about an idea you believed in. How did you respond, and what strategies did you use to persevere and continue advocating for your vision?

3. If you already have a supportive network, in what ways can you leverage it to help you navigate institutional challenges? How can you use it to champion others and their good ideas?

---

1. Zanes, Warren, "Tom Petty Reveals Struggles With Heroin, Abuse, and Heartbreak in Must-Read Biography: Exclusive Excerpts," *Billboard*, November 5, 2015, https://www.billboard.com/music/features/tom-petty-biography-struggles-heroin-abuse-heartbreak-6753771/.

CHAPTER 2

Finding the Right Fit
Jimi Hendrix and The Monkees

I'll keep this world from draggin' me down. Gonna stand my ground. And I won't back down.

Tom Petty

In the summer of 1967, an unexpected musical pairing took place that would become a legendary story in rock history. Jimi Hendrix, an emerging guitar virtuoso, joined The Monkees, a popular American television band, as their opening act.[1]

What followed was a fascinating clash of musical genres and fan expectations, culminating in Hendrix being booed off the stage and criticized for not being good enough to precede The Monkees—a moment that now stands as a curious footnote in the annals of rock history. Yet it also became a pivotal moment that showcased Hendrix's resilience and determination to stay true to his artistic vision.

A Clash of Cultures

The Monkees were at the height of their fame in 1967. Known for their television show and catchy pop hits, they had garnered a massive following, particularly among teenagers. Their music, though often dismissed by critics as manufactured, resonated with a broad audience. On the other hand, Jimi Hendrix was a rising star in the rock and blues scenes, known for his innovative guitar playing, psychedelic sound, and electrifying performances.

The decision to have Hendrix open for The Monkees was both bold and bewildering. The idea reportedly came from Micky Dolenz of The Monkees who had seen Hendrix perform in New York and was blown away by his talent. Dolenz and the rest of The Monkees were fans of Hendrix's music and wanted to expose their audience to his groundbreaking sound. However, the musical styles of Hendrix and The Monkees were worlds apart, setting the stage for a clash of cultures.

Booed Off Stage

The tour kicked off in Jacksonville, Florida, on July 8, 1967. Hendrix's performances were a stark contrast to what The Monkees' fans were accustomed to. His sets were loud, raw, and filled with extended guitar solos and bluesy improvisations. He performed songs like "Purple Haze," "Foxy Lady," and "Hey Joe," which were unfamiliar to the young fans of The Monkees who came for bubblegum pop and light-hearted entertainment.

From the beginning, it was clear that the pairing was not a natural fit. The Monkees' predominantly teenage fan base found Hendrix's music jarring and his stage antics bewildering. Hendrix, known for playing his guitar with his teeth and setting it on fire, was too wild and intense for the young crowd. Many in the audience were there with their parents who were even less appreciative of Hendrix's revolutionary approach to rock music.

The defining moment of this mismatch came in Forest Hills, New York, on July 14, 1967. During one of his performances, Hendrix was met with boos and jeers from the audience. Frustrated and disheartened, he flipped his guitar around, gave the crowd the finger, and walked off stage. The incident was a public humiliation for Hendrix, and it highlighted the vast chasm between his innovative artistry and The Monkees' mainstream appeal.

Mental Fortitude and Focus

Despite the negative reception during the tour, Hendrix's resolve did not waver. Instead of succumbing to the criticism, he used it as fuel to drive his artistic journey forward. Hendrix had always been an introspective individual, and this experience forced him to reflect deeply on his music and his place in the industry. He sought solace in the support of his bandmates, Mitch Mitchell and Noel Redding, who believed in his vision and helped him stay focused.

Hendrix turned to his guitar, the instrument that had always been his sanctuary. He spent hours practicing, experimenting with new sounds, and perfecting his craft. The rejection he faced only reinforced his belief in staying true to his unique style, no matter how unconventional it seemed. He understood that breaking new ground often came with resistance, but he was determined to push through and make his mark.

The tour continued for a few more shows, but the writing was on the wall. Hendrix and his management decided to leave the tour after only seven performances. The experience of facing criticism and rejection in front of thousands was a sobering one for Hendrix. For The Monkees, it was a lesson in the unpredictability of musical pairings and the importance of understanding one's audience.

However, Hendrix's departure from the tour marked the beginning of a new chapter. Free from the constraints of a bad fit, he poured his energy into his own music. Just months later, he released the album, *Axis: Bold as Love*, which received critical acclaim and solidified his reputation as a pioneering artist.

My Personal Journey

When I was a young administrator with dreams of one day becoming a principal, my superintendent once told me something that cut me to my core. He said, "I just don't see you as a principal." It felt like a blow to all the hard work, passion, and dedication I had poured into my career, not to mention all the changes I made in my personal life to meet the district's needs.

Clearly, my superintendent and I had different educational philosophies, different leadership styles, and different ideas about what it meant to be an administrator, but at that time, I didn't filter his words through that lens. Instead, his perspective felt like a rejection of who I was. It made me question whether I'd ever be the right fit.

But now, looking back, I realize this rejection was one of the best things that could have happened to me. In fact, I'm thankful I didn't get the job back then. That disappointment, as painful as it was, forced me to reflect deeply on who I was as an educator and a leader. Had I stayed in that system, I might have been confined by expectations that didn't align with my values or my vision for education.

Instead, that rejection pushed me to search for environments that would embrace my style, my approach to leadership, and my philosophy on what a school community should look like. And when I found those places, I flourished.

This was one of those experiences that shaped me into the leader I am today—one who believes in the power of community, technology, collaboration, and most importantly, seeing each person's potential.

Lessons for Educators

My experience, like the story of Jimi Hendrix's experience as an opening act for The Monkees, vividly illustrates the importance of finding the right environment to showcase your talents. For school leaders and teachers, this lesson is particularly pertinent. Too often, educators struggle with feelings of inadequacy and imposter syndrome when, in reality, they may simply be in the wrong environment—one that does not recognize or appreciate their unique skill sets.

Below are four ways to put this lesson to work for you:

1. **Embrace mismatched opportunities as stepping stones.** Just as Jimi Hendrix's experience with The Monkees highlighted a misalignment, you too may find yourself in roles or settings that don't reflect your strengths or style. Try to view these experiences not as failures but as clarifying steps toward understanding where your work truly belongs.

2. **Seek environments that align with your values and talents.** Hendrix's journey reminds us of the importance of fit. His talent resonated not with The Monkees' fans but in spaces that celebrated his groundbreaking sound. Research and find an environment that aligns with your teaching philosophy that will enable you to make a more profound impact.

3. **Reflect on criticism as a tool for growth, not a measure of worth.** Facing boos from an ill-matched audience didn't stop Hendrix; instead, he used the

experience to refine his artistry and strengthen his resolve. You too can use feedback, even if it's disheartening, to further hone your skills and affirm your commitment to your goals.

4. **Recognize the role of resilience in professional fulfillment.** Hendrix's resilience and determination to stay true to his vision serve as powerful reminders for educators navigating setbacks. Work to strengthen your resilience so you can use each obstacle to build a stronger foundation for success.

Write Your Own Lyrics

1. Reflect on a time when you felt out of place or unappreciated in your teaching environment. What were the key factors that contributed to those feelings, and how did you navigate that experience?

2. What specific qualities or characteristics do you look for in a school environment that aligns with your teaching philosophy and values? How can you identify and seek out such environments?

3. Think about a time recently when you received discouraging criticism. How can you transform that into useful feedback to deepen your skills, build up your resilience, and recommit to your priorities?

1. Pesant, Steven C., "Hey, Hey, We're the . . . Experience? How the Jimi Hendrix Experience Landed on Tour with The Monkees," Sony Music Entertainment, October 27, 2023, https://www.jimihendrix.com/editorial/hey-hey-were-the-experience/.

CHAPTER 3

The Long Road to Success
The Allman Brothers Band

You owe it to yourself to express yourself and not someone else.

Duane Allman

Success is rarely a straight, easy path. It is often a winding road filled with twists, turns, and detours. The story of The Allman Brothers Band is a perfect illustration of this journey. Their tale is not just one of musical genius but of perseverance, resilience, and the relentless pursuit of a dream.[1] Their story offers profound insights for anyone striving to find their place and achieve success.

The Early Struggles

Before the formation of The Allman Brothers Band, Duane and Gregg Allman were no strangers to rejection and frustration. Their early bands, such as The Allman Joys and The Hour Glass, faced numerous setbacks. Despite their talent and dedication, these groups struggled to find their footing in the competitive music industry.

The Hour Glass, signed to Liberty Records, faced particular disappointment. The label failed to support them adequately, leading to low album sales and eventual disbandment.

In these early years, the would-be Allman brothers experienced the harsh realities of the music business. Yet these challenges did not deter them. Instead, they honed their craft, learning valuable lessons from each disappointment. They understood that rejection was not a reflection of their talent but a step in their journey toward finding the right platform for their music.

Formation of The Allman Brothers Band

The turning point came in 1969 when Duane Allman assembled a group of like-minded musicians, leading to the formation of The Allman Brothers Band. This ensemble included talented artists like Dickey Betts, Berry Oakley, Butch Trucks, and Jai Johanny Johanson. Together, they created a unique blend of rock, blues, jazz, and country that would eventually define Southern rock.

Even with this new band, success was not immediate, however. They played hundreds of gigs, often for meager pay, and faced continued skepticism from the industry. However, their relentless pursuit of excellence and their distinctive sound began to attract a dedicated following.

The band's big break came when they caught the attention of Phil Walden and Frank Fenter of Capricorn Records, a subsidiary of Atlantic Records. This partnership provided the support and platform they needed to reach a broader audience.

Breakthrough and Legacy

With Capricorn Records, The Allman Brothers Band released their self-titled debut album in 1969. Although it did not achieve immediate commercial success, it laid the groundwork for what was to come. Their relentless touring and dynamic live performances earned them a loyal fan base. The release of their landmark album, *At Fillmore East*, in 1971 cemented their status as one of the most influential bands in rock history.

The Allman Brothers Band's journey from obscurity to stardom was marked by perseverance, patience, and a steadfast belief in their music. They faced numerous obstacles, but their commitment to their craft and their ability to adapt and grow ultimately led to their success.

My Personal Journey

Fresh out of college and ready to find my first full-time job, I sought a position in a district where I had once been a student. After three rounds of interviews, I was thrilled to hear I was the top candidate. We discussed salary, benefits, and all the details. All that was left was one final step—getting the board of education's approval.

I eagerly awaited the call after the board meeting but, to my dismay, it never came. When I followed up two days later, I learned the board had gone in a different direction, hiring a friend's daughter instead. It was a tough lesson in how politics and personal connections can influence decisions.

But that rejection turned out to be a blessing. It pushed me to explore other opportunities, and I landed a full-time teaching position in a new area of the state where I knew no one. The move was intimidating, but it forced me to adapt, build connections, and establish myself in this unfamiliar environment.

The experience showed me that the road to success is often long and may include a journey into the unknown. It requires patience, courage, and stamina, not to mention adaptability and a sense of adventure.

It also taught me the importance of transparency and frankness in the hiring process—something I have carried with me into my role as an administrator—ensuring candidates understand that nothing is truly final until a school board makes its decision.

Lessons for Educators

The story of The Allman Brothers Band as well as my own experience hold a valuable lesson: Success takes time and steadfastness. They are reminders to embrace your own journey, to learn from your hardships, and to stay committed to your dreams. In the end, finding the right place to be successful is not just about talent but about resilience, adaptability, and unwavering determination.

Here are a few ways to apply these lessons to your situation:

1. **Embrace the journey**. Don't expect the road to success to be short and smooth. Setbacks along the way are an inevitable part of the journey. Receive each one as an opportunity to learn, grow, and gain strength.

2. **Stay committed to your vision**. The Allman brothers never wavered in their commitment to their music. They believed in their unique sound and pursued it relentlessly, even when success seemed elusive. Resist

the pressure to set aside your values or abandon your dreams for the sake of what others define as success.

3. **Be prepared to adapt and evolve**. The transition from their earlier bands to The Allman Brothers Band demonstrates the importance of adaptability. Finding the right platform for your talents often requires flexibility and a willingness to explore unconventional or creative alternatives.

4. **Persevere through challenges**. The Allman Brothers Band's story is a testament to the power of perseverance and the importance of staying the course, even in the face of adversity. In your own journey, expect challenges and plan for them ahead of time so they don't derail your progress.

Write Your Own Lyrics

1. Reflect on a time when you faced a long and arduous journey in your teaching career. How did you persevere when you felt worn out or discouraged? What lessons did you learn that helped you grow as an educator?

2. In what ways can you stay committed to your vision for education, even when immediate success seems elusive? How can you ensure that your unique teaching style and philosophy remain a guiding force in your professional journey?

3. How can you adapt and evolve in your teaching practices to better align with the needs of your students and the educational environment? What might be some creative ways to implement necessary changes?

1. "The Allman Brothers Band: Innovation and Freedom," The Denver Folklore Center, accessed December 5, 2024, https://www.denverfolklore.com/module/news/10330/the-allman-brothers-band-innovation-and-freedom/.

CHAPTER 4

Enduring Repeated Rejections
The Beatles

Despite everything, no one can dictate who you are to other people.

Prince

Some artists are lucky enough to face only one major setback before finding success. Many others, however, are hit with rejection over and over again to the point that most people would give up.

Take, for instance, the fact that The Beatles endured repeated rejections on their journey from obscurity to global superstardom.[1] Their tenacity in the face of these defeats offers invaluable lessons on the power of mental stamina and the importance of unwavering belief.

Turned Away by Many

The Beatles, now revered as one of the most influential bands in history, were not always the icons we know today. Before their rise to fame, they faced numerous rejections that could have easily discouraged them. The band was turned away by several recording companies, including Columbia, HMV, Pye, Philips, and Oriole.

Perhaps the most infamous of these was Decca Records. After listening to their demo, Decca executives famously declared (which has since been denied by executive Dick Rowe) that "guitar groups are on the way out" and that "The Beatles have no future in show business."[2]

This rejection was a significant blow, especially for Pete Best who left the group shortly after. But it did not deter John Lennon, Paul McCartney, and George Harrison from moving forward. After bringing in Ringo Starr to replace Best, they continued to write music and perform whenever and wherever they could.

Their persistence paid off when they caught the attention of George Martin at EMI's Parlophone label who signed them on June 6, 1962. Under his guidance, The Beatles transformed into the groundbreaking band that would go on to change the music industry forever.

My Personal Journey

My professional journey toward becoming a building-level principal has been shaped by multiple rejections. Eight, to be exact. On eight separate occasions, I stood as a finalist for school principal positions, each time believing that my goal was within reach, only to face the painful reality of being turned away.

The sting of coming so close, only to be denied, was overwhelming. Each rejection carried with it a heavy weight of disappointment and stress, making me question my path, my abilities, and whether I was truly meant to lead.

I vividly remember calling each superintendent after being passed over. Some were gracious enough to speak with me while others didn't respond. For the most part, the reasons they gave for my rejection were beyond my control: They wanted to hire from within, they promised a friend a job, they were looking for someone more diverse, and, in one instance, I was seen as too intimidating to the team.

In some ways, it was a relief to learn that these decisions had little to do with my credentials or qualifications—they were about team dynamics, internal preferences, or other factors unrelated to me. On the other hand, that meant I could only control certain aspects of my career advancement. I'd have to let go of what was out of my hands and focus instead on what I could control, which is easier said than done. Finally, on my ninth try, I was selected to become a building principal, and how fortunate I am that I landed where I did. Becoming a new principal in a new district wasn't easy at first, but all the experiences I encountered there pushed me to become a better leader.

Lessons for Educators

The philosophy of *Amor Fati*, which translates to "love of fate," encourages us to embrace everything that happens in our lives, including the hardships and rejections. This Stoic principle teaches us to see every event as necessary and beneficial, no matter how difficult it may seem at the time.[3]

For The Beatles, the rejection from Decca Records was a pivotal moment that redirected them toward a better path. For me, being passed over for eight principal positions was a period of trial that prepared me for the right opportunity.

One rejection is hard enough, but repeated ones can feel like an insurmountable roadblock. However, when one direction is impassable, it's often an indication it's time to redirect. It's an opportunity to explore a path that we might not have considered otherwise.

Below are a few ways to implement these lessons:

1. **Build mental stamina.** Despite numerous rejections, The Beatles never wavered in their belief in their music. Similarly, developing the mental and emotional fortitude to keep going is crucial to outlasting the naysayers.

2. **Learn to make adjustments.** Every rejection is an opportunity to pause and reevaluate. Use these experiences to refine your approach, adjust your plans, improve your skills, and gain new insights.

3. **Embrace *Amor Fati*.** Learn to accept and love your fate, including the setbacks. Trust that each event is part of a larger plan that will ultimately lead you to where you are meant to be.

4. **Explore a different direction.** Understand that rejection is not an endpoint but a pivot point, guiding you toward better opportunities that align more closely with your true path. Seize the chance to explore other options and possibilities.

Write Your Own Lyrics

1. Have you ever been rejected more than once? If so, what gave you the strength to keep trying? If not, how might you mentally and emotionally prepare for the possibility of repeated rejections down the road?

2. In what ways can you apply the philosophy of *Amor Fati* to your current professional journey? How can embracing

both successes and failures shape your approach to personal and professional growth?

3. Think about a time in your career when your path was blocked and you had to go in a different direction. How did you adjust your plans and expectations? Did exploring other options end up leading you to a better path? Why or why not?

---

1. Shoemaker, Paul J. H., "Love Me Do: Management Lessons from the Fifth Beatle," *Knowledge at Wharton*, March 18, 2016, https://knowledge.wharton.upenn.edu/article/love-management-lessons-fifth-beatle/.

2. Quote Investigator, "Beatles Rejection: We Don't Like Their Sound. Groups of Guitars Are On Their Way Out," April 27, 2013, https://quoteinvestigator.com/2013/04/27/guitars-out/.

3. "Amor Fati: The Formula for Human Greatness," Daily Stoic, accessed November 6, 2024, https://dailystoic.com/amor-fati-love-of-fate/.

CHAPTER 5

The Importance of Mentorship

Eazy-E and Dr. Dre

There are no roadblocks, only springboards.

Brent Smith

Eric Lynn Wright, known to the world as Eazy-E, was more than just a rapper; he was a pioneer, a visionary, and the godfather of gangsta rap. However, before he donned his signature Raiders cap and delivered raw, unfiltered tales of Compton life, Wright was a young man burdened with self-doubt. In a world where belief in oneself is paramount, Eazy-E found an unexpected source of support and mentorship in Dr. Dre, a fellow artist who saw his potential long before he did.

Eazy-E's entry into the music industry was far from conventional. Originally a drug dealer, he used his earnings to fund a record label, Ruthless Records. Despite his entrepreneurial spirit, Eazy-E didn't see himself as a rapper. His raspy voice and lack of formal musical training made him question his place in the rap world. Yet it was precisely these raw qualities that Dr. Dre recognized as authentic and marketable.[1]

Dr. Dre: The Mentor

Dr. Dre, a member of the World Class Wreckin' Cru, was a talented DJ and producer with an ear for groundbreaking sounds. When he met Eazy-E, he saw beyond the rough exterior and heard the potential for something revolutionary. Dre's belief in Eazy-E's unique voice and perspective was steadfast. He encouraged Eazy-E to step behind the mic, coaching him through recording sessions and refining his delivery.

With Dre's guidance, Eazy-E recorded "Boyz-n-the-Hood," a track that would become a cornerstone of gangsta rap. Despite Eazy-E's initial reluctance, the song's success was undeniable. Together with Ice Cube, MC Ren, DJ Yella, and Dr. Dre, Eazy-E formed N.W.A., a group that would redefine the rap genre and bring the harsh realities of inner-city life to mainstream America.

My Personal Journey

As a young teacher, I struggled with finding the right mentor to help me navigate the complexities of the classroom and develop as a leader. Many times, I had questions and faced rejections, yet I had little guidance. While there were people around who offered help, I never found a close enough connection with someone who could provide the deep support and wisdom I needed. The lack of mentorship left me feeling uncertain and isolated, especially as I tried to grow in a profession that demands both expertise and resilience.

In those early years, I began seeking out resources on my own. Social media became a lifeline, offering access to a broader community of educators and leaders who shared their insights and experiences. Leadership books and podcasts were also a cornerstone of my development, helping me build a foundation in leadership when I didn't have mentors that I could meet with in person.

Eventually, I was fortunate enough to find truly remarkable mentors who transformed my career. People like Michael Curran, Peter Brandt, Bob Garguilo, Janice Fipp, Scott Rocco, Phil Heery, Nick Polyak, Mike Lubelfeld, Jon Bartelt, Pam Moran, Bill Ziegler, Bobby Dodd, Winston Sakurai, David Culberhouse, David Jakes, Cheryl Simone, Kirk Koennecke, Brad Black, my amazing wife, Abigail, and others all played pivotal roles in shaping my understanding of leadership and guiding me through challenges. They didn't just offer advice; they invested in my growth, helping me become a better educator and a stronger leader.

Additionally, I found reverse mentors in the students, teachers, and aspiring superintendents I worked with in mentorship programs. These experiences taught me the power of learning from others, regardless of their position or experience level. They helped me stay grounded, challenged my thinking, and expanded my perspective on what it means to lead.

Mentorship transformed my career in profound ways. It taught me the importance of paying it forward and ensuring that, as a leader, I am intentional about providing the same level of support and guidance that I was so fortunate to receive. It's a reminder that none of us succeed in isolation—it's the relationships we build along the way that make all the difference.

Lessons for Educators

Eazy-E's rise to fame was not just a testament to his talent but also to the power of mentorship. Dr. Dre's unwavering support and belief in Eazy-E's abilities were crucial in helping him overcome his self-doubt.

This dynamic mirrors the experiences of many educators who struggle with imposter syndrome, feeling inadequate despite their qualifications and accomplishments. With the right mentorship and a belief in their unique capabilities, educators can overcome self-doubt and achieve extraordinary success.

Here are some practical ways to do just that:

1. **Look for mentors in unexpected places.** Eazy-E found a powerful mentor in another artist who could've easily been his rival. I found guidance from people through social media, books, and podcasts. Seek mentors who believe in your potential, even if that means finding them in unconventional ways.

2. **Listen to those who believe in you.** Eazy-E's journey was fraught with self-doubt, but he managed to tune that out and instead listen to the voice of someone who believed in him. Remember that self-doubt is a common hurdle, not an insurmountable barrier. Downplay your internal critic and focus on the encouragement and guidance of those who support you.

3. **Celebrate small wins**. Every successful recording session and hit song was a step forward for Eazy-E. Likewise, you should celebrate your achievements, no matter how small, to build confidence and momentum.

4. **Pay it forward.** Instead of waiting for them to ask, offer support to colleagues and employees who are struggling. You might end up being just the kind of mentor they need at that time, and in the process, you'll discover you're learning valuable lessons from them too.

Write Your Own Lyrics

1. Reflect on a time when a mentor provided you with crucial guidance or encouragement. How did their belief in your abilities impact your confidence and performance in your role?

2. What are some of your most recent wins—big or small? Have you paused to celebrate them? If so, how did that boost your self-confidence? If not, now is a great time to recognize those accomplishments.

3. Think about a colleague or employee who might be struggling with self-doubt or imposter syndrome. What steps can you take to offer them support, wisdom, and reassurance to help them recognize and reach their full potential?

---

1. Heasman, Chris, "Eazy-E's Tragic Real-Life Story," Grunge, February 3, 2023, https://www.grunge.com/130120/eazy-es-tragic-real-life-story/.

CHAPTER 6

Innovating and Evolving
Miles Davis

I'd rather regret doing something than not doing something.

James Hetfield

M iles Davis, a name synonymous with innovation in jazz, was never content with the status quo. Over a career spanning five decades, Davis continually reinvented his music, pushing the boundaries of jazz and influencing artists across genres.

His journey was one of constant evolution, characterized by a fearless approach to change and a relentless pursuit of excellence. Each reinvention marked a departure from the previous one, and with every new direction, Davis not only reshaped the landscape of jazz but also faced a significant amount of resistance, especially from critics who were sometimes unable or unwilling to understand his vision.[1]

Ever-Evolving Genius

From his early days with bebop to his groundbreaking work in cool jazz, modal jazz, and fusion, Miles Davis was a master of reinvention. Each phase of his career reflected a deep commitment to exploring new musical landscapes.

In the 1950s, Davis's *Birth of the Cool* sessions marked the emergence of cool jazz, a departure from the frenetic pace of bebop. The late 1950s and early 1960s saw him pioneer modal jazz with the iconic album, *Kind of Blue*, which simplified harmonic structures to allow for greater melodic freedom.

Kind of Blue became one of the best-selling jazz albums of all time and is widely regarded as a masterpiece, but even it wasn't immune to criticism in its time. Some critics, especially those who were deeply entrenched in traditional jazz forms, didn't immediately embrace the album's departure from complex chord progressions. There were those who felt it was too simplistic or even too abstract for the time.

The late 1960s and 1970s brought another dramatic shift as Davis embraced electric instruments and rock influences, resulting in the seminal album, *Bitches Brew*, and the birth of jazz fusion. *Bitches Brew* received mixed reviews initially, with some critics praising its boldness and others condemning it as noise. Even within the jazz community, there was a backlash against the incorporation of electric instruments and rock rhythms into what was once considered a sacred art form.[2]

Each transformation was met with both acclaim and criticism, but Davis remained undeterred, always looking forward and never resting on past successes or dwelling on earlier setbacks.

My Personal Journey

Reflecting on my journey, it's clear that the transition from assistant principal to principal was not as seamless as I anticipated. Many of the approaches and strategies that brought success in one role were no longer effective in the next. Each district had its own culture, expectations, and challenges; methods that had worked before became outdated. It was obvious that relying on past successes would not be enough.

When I stepped into the role of principal, I realized I needed to adapt to new leadership dynamics and take on a broader perspective. The skills I honed in previous positions were valuable, but I had to recalibrate my approach to meet the unique demands of each school and district I went to.

This pattern repeated itself when I moved into a superintendent role. Suddenly, my responsibilities were more complex, and my previous leadership style needed to evolve once again.

The volatile, uncertain, complex, and ambiguous (VUCA)[3] world of modern education demanded constant innovation and adaptation. What worked in one place, or even a year before, wasn't guaranteed to succeed in another. As I transitioned between superintendent positions, I learned that no two districts operated in the same way. I had to be agile—willing to discard old ideas and embrace new strategies that aligned with a changing educational landscape.

Lessons for Educators

Davis's legacy offers invaluable lessons on the importance of resourcefulness and innovation, as does my educational leadership journey. The world of education today is a VUCA landscape, characterized by rapid changes in technology, shifting societal expectations, and evolving educational standards. Educators must navigate these complexities while preparing students for a future that is equally unpredictable.

Consider the following ways to stay current and innovative in your teaching.

1. **Embrace change**. Like Miles Davis, educators should view change not as a threat, but as an opportunity. The ability to adapt to new technologies, pedagogical approaches, and student needs is crucial in a VUCA environment. This mindset fosters resilience and opens the door to innovative solutions.

2. **Take risks**. Davis was never afraid to take risks, even if it meant alienating some of his audience. Educators, too, must be willing to experiment with new teaching methods and curricula. Taking risks can lead to breakthroughs in student engagement and learning outcomes, setting higher standards for the entire school community.

3. **Pursue excellence relentlessly**. Davis's commitment to excellence was unwavering. He pushed himself and his collaborators to achieve higher levels of artistry. Similarly, educators should strive for continuous improvement, seeking out professional development opportunities and staying abreast of the latest educational research.

4. **Collaborate to innovate**. Davis's collaborations with other musicians were pivotal in his creative process. You too can benefit from collaborating with colleagues, sharing best practices, and fostering a culture of co-creation within your school. These efforts can lead to the development of interdisciplinary curricula and new strategies to enhance student learning.

Write Your Own Lyrics

1. Reflect on a time when you significantly changed your teaching approach or curriculum. What inspired this change? What were the outcomes for you and your students?

2. Think of a risk you took in your educational practice that led to a breakthrough in student engagement or learning outcomes. How did this experience shape your approach to teaching?

3. Consider a successful collaboration you have had with colleagues. What made this collaboration effective, and how did it impact your teaching and student learning? How can you foster more collaborative innovation within your school community?

---

1. Early, Gerald, "Miles Davis, Style Beyond Style," *The Common Reader: A Journal of the Essay*, September 29, 2021, https://commonreader.wustl.edu/miles-davis-style-beyond-style/.

2. "Miles Davis," Biography.com, May 24, 2021, https://www.biography.com/musicians/miles-davis/.

3. U.S. Army Heritage and Education Center, "Who first originated the term VUCA (Volatility, Uncertainty, Complexity and Ambiguity?" U.S. Army War College, December 6, 2022, https://usawc.libanswers.com/faq/84869/.

CHAPTER 7

Overcoming Hardship
Johnny Cash

For every dark night, there's a brighter day.

Tupac

Johnny Cash, one of the most influential musicians of the 20th century, wasn't born into fame and fortune. His early life was marked by poverty, hardship, and rejection.

Born in Kingsland, Arkansas, in 1932, Cash grew up during the Great Depression. His family worked long hours in cotton fields and, like many others, struggled to make ends meet.[1] Despite the bleak circumstances, young Johnny found solace in music, inspired by the hymns his mother sang and the radio broadcasts he avidly listened to.

After serving in the Air Force, he married his first wife, Vivian Liberto, and moved to Memphis, Tennessee, to pursue a music career. There he faced numerous rejections from record labels and endured long periods of financial instability.

Early auditions at Sun Records, where he performed gospel music, were met with skepticism. Sam Phillips, Sun Records' founder, famously told him, "Go home and sin, then come back with a song I can sell."

Becoming "The Man in Black"

Despite these rejections, Cash didn't give up. He took Phillips' advice to heart, returning with original songs that reflected his gritty life experiences and unique voice. His persistence paid off when he recorded "Cry! Cry! Cry!" and "Hey Porter," which caught the public's attention and marked the beginning of his rise to fame.[2]

Even after achieving success, Cash faced personal and professional challenges, including battles with addiction and turbulent relationships. Yet, through it all, he remained dedicated to his craft, continuing to create timeless music that resonated with millions.

In wrestling with his own demons, he aligned himself with music fans who were rejected by society and commiserated with their sadness, resentment, and hopelessness. His authenticity, raw emotion, unyielding spirit—and of course, dressing like he was attending a funeral—became his trademarks, earning Cash the moniker, "The Man in Black."

My Personal Journey

Growing up, I often heard my family motto repeated like gospel: "Want to wreck a good man? Send him to college." In our blue-collar world, success wasn't defined by degrees or diplomas but by grit, sweat, and resilience. My family ran a water well drilling business where long hours in the blistering summer sun and frigid winter air weren't just a rite of passage—they were a way of life. Education, while valued, wasn't seen as a necessity for success. Yet, against this backdrop, I found myself drawn to a different path.

College was my escape and my gamble, but it came with a steep price—$60,000 in student loan debt at an unforgiving eight percent interest rate. With a starting teaching salary of just $36,000, I was barely making enough to cover basic expenses, let alone chip away at my debt.

To make matters worse, I needed reliable transportation to get to and from work, so I bought my first truck, adding thousands more to my financial burden. When I decided to enroll in a master's program after my first year of teaching, the costs ballooned further, pushing the grand total over $100,000.

The pressure was immense but so was my resolve. I refused to let these numbers define me or derail the future I envisioned.

For four years, I lived a life of disciplined frugality. I had little to no social life, spent weekends triple couponing at the grocery store, and celebrated small victories when I could afford a night out or a minor indulgence. By sheer determination and relentless budgeting, I paid off every cent. The lessons learned during those lean years—tenacity, resourcefulness, and the ability to persevere through numerous hardships—became my armor.

Like Johnny Cash, I wasn't handed success. I had to earn it with calloused hands, a stoic mindset, and unrelenting determination.

Lessons for Educators

Many educators today can relate to Johnny Cash's story of overcoming adversity or my story of paying off debt. Obstacles like growing up in challenging environments, facing economic hardships, and battling addiction can create a daunting path.

However, just as Cash's perseverance led him to success, you can draw strength from your past and use it as a foundation for building a brighter future for yourself and your students.

Below are some steps you can take to get there:

1. **Embrace your roots**. Johnny Cash's music was deeply rooted in his life experiences. Likewise, you can draw from your background and use your unique perspective to connect with students and foster a supportive and inclusive learning environment.

2. **Practice authenticity.** Cash's authenticity was a significant factor in his popularity among people at the margins of society. Being genuine and true to yourself helps to build stronger relationships with your students and colleagues because it fosters trust and synergy.

3. **Turn pain into power**. Cash's ability to channel his struggles into his music made his work deeply impactful. Similarly, you can turn personal shortcomings and professional failures into sources of inspiration and empathy.

4. **Set an example.** When you endure through tough times, you set an example for your peers and employees, even your supervisor. Plus, personal stories of overcoming hardship and rejection can inspire and motivate students facing their own challenges.

Write Your Own Lyrics

1. How have your personal struggles and professional challenges shaped your journey as an educator, and how can you use these experiences to inspire and motivate

your students?

2. In what ways can you become more authentic in your teaching practice, and how might this authenticity strengthen your relationships with students and colleagues?

3. Think about a hardship in your life you had to overcome to get where you are now. How can you leverage that experience to make a greater impact at your school? Is there someone in particular who might benefit from hearing your story?

---

1. Piccotti, Tyler, "Johnny Cash," Biography.com, May 28, 2024, https://www.biography.com/musicians/johnny-cash/.

2. Danker, Fred, "Johnny Cash," Country Music Hall of Fame, accessed December 11, 2024, https://www.countrymusichalloffame.org/hall-of-fame/johnny-cash/.

CHAPTER 8

The Struggle for Recognition
Bob Dylan

Be your own artist, and always be confident in what you're doing. If you're not going to be confident, you might as well not be doing it.

Aretha Franklin

B ob Dylan, a name now synonymous with musical genius and lyrical mastery, wasn't always celebrated by the industry. In the early stages of his career Dylan faced numerous rejections and a lack of formal recognition. His unique voice and unconventional style didn't fit neatly into the industry's expectations, and this initially hindered his ability to garner awards and accolades. However, Dylan's story is one of resilience, persistence, and the power of redirection.

Uncelebrated Beginnings

When Dylan burst onto the music scene in the early 1960s, his raw and raspy voice, combined with his poignant and often political lyrics, set him apart.[1] However, this distinctiveness also led to many rejections. Critics were divided, and award bodies largely overlooked his early works. Albums like *The Freewheelin' Bob Dylan* and *Bringing It All Back Home*, which are now considered masterpieces, didn't receive the accolades they deserved at the time.

Despite this lack of recognition, Dylan continued to write and perform, driven by a deeper purpose and a belief in his artistic vision. He turned the industry's rejection into fuel for his creativity, pushing the boundaries of folk, rock, and blues.

The Turning Point

Dylan's tenacity eventually paid off. His ability to redirect his frustrations into creative energy led to a string of groundbreaking albums in the mid-1960s, including *Highway 61 Revisited* and *Blonde on Blonde*. These works solidified his status as a musical pioneer, and the accolades began to follow.

Over time, Dylan won numerous Grammy Awards, including a Lifetime Achievement Award, and in 2016, he was awarded the Nobel Prize in Literature, recognizing his profound impact on music and culture.[2]

My Personal Journey

Writing nominations for others is a truly rewarding journey. When I take time to highlight someone's contributions, I'm not just listing their achievements—I'm reflecting on how much they mean to our community and to me. Each nomination is a way of honoring their voice and their work, aiming to show others the depth of their impact. There's a quiet but powerful hope in the process—that those who've given so much will see just how valued they are.

When these nominations don't lead to recognition, it can feel disheartening, especially when I know how much these educators have done and how much they deserve. But I remind myself that real value doesn't rest in titles or awards. In writing these nominations, I'm creating a lasting record of their contributions and the qualities that make them special. Whether it's recognized publicly or not, their impact endures in the lives they've touched.

Sometimes, the most deserving people are those whose work isn't flashy or easily quantified but is deeply transformative. Their influence goes beyond simple metrics or accolades, and the passing over of their nomination shows the limits of traditional recognition. This reminds me that leadership isn't about the trophies on display; it's about the quiet, steady difference one makes, often without applause.

When someone I've nominated doesn't receive recognition, it also pushes me to think about how I can celebrate my colleagues and employees more personally. Am I expressing appreciation enough in the small moments? Am I making sure their efforts are seen and valued every day, even if it's just between us? These are the quieter forms of acknowledgment, the ones that matter most in the long run.

In the end, being overlooked for an award doesn't lessen a person's worth. Their work, their integrity, and their genuine impact carry a significance far deeper than any title could capture.

Lessons for Educators

Much like Bob Dylan, many educators struggle to get the recognition they deserve despite their hard work and dedication. They are often passed over for promotions, awards, and accolades, leading to frustration and self-doubt. However, in this is a powerful lesson: A lack of recognition can be an opportunity for creativity and ingenuity.

1. **Find a work-around.** Dylan constantly evolved his music, blending different genres and experimenting with new sounds, which eventually paid off. If your talent and achievements are frequently overlooked, explore new ways to present yourself and highlight your contributions. It might just be a matter of outwitting the algorithms, if you will.

2. **Celebrate your own impact**. Awards and recognition are not the only measures of success. Dylan's impact on music and culture extends far beyond his trophy shelf. Remember that your influence on students' lives is profound and lasting, even if it isn't always formally acknowledged.

3. **Be patient.** Just as Dylan's persistence eventually led to widespread acclaim, your efforts will eventually be recognized. This recognition may come in various forms, from formal awards to the heartfelt gratitude of students and parents, but be patient. It will happen.

4. **Speak up for others.** If you've been passed over for a well-deserved recognition, you know the discouragement it causes. Look around your school for others who are quietly doing meaningful work without getting any acclaim, and make their contributions known.

Write Your Own Lyrics

1. Reflect on a time in your teaching career when you were overlooked for a promotion, award, or other recognition. How did you respond, and did that response have the

desired result? Why or why not?

2. Think about a time when the impact of your teaching was recognized in a nontraditional or intangible way such as a student's success or a heartfelt thank you from a parent. How did this influence your view of formal recognition and your sense of professional fulfillment?

3. Is there a fellow teacher or staff member at your school who deserves recognition they haven't yet received? What can you do to celebrate them and show appreciation for their hard work and contributions?

---

1. "Bob Dylan," Biography.com, April 13, 2021, https://www.biography.com/musicians/bob-dylan/.

2. Herrak, Akram, "Bob Dylan's Odyssey: A Deep Dive Into the Life of a Music Legend," The Collector, May 12, 2024, https://www.thecollector.com/bob-dylan-years-genres/.

CHAPTER 9

Taking a Different Path
Elvis Presley

Tomorrow belongs to those who can hear it coming.
David Bowie

E lvis Presley, known worldwide as the "King of Rock 'n' Roll," wasn't always a music legend. Born in Tupelo, Mississippi, in 1935, Elvis came from humble beginnings. His family faced financial struggles, and Elvis took various jobs to help make ends meet. One of these jobs was as a truck driver, a profession he held while nurturing dreams of a music career.[1]

The Grand Ole Opry Rejection

In 1954, Elvis had his big break—or so he thought—when he performed at the Grand Ole Opry, the prestigious country music stage in Nashville. Despite his burgeoning talent and unique sound, his performance did not receive the acclaim he had hoped for. After his show, Jim Denny, the manager of the Grand Ole Opry, famously told him, "You ain't goin' nowhere, son. You ought to go back to driving a truck."

This harsh rejection could have crushed his spirit. Instead, it became a defining moment in his career. Rather than giving up, Elvis took this rejection as fuel to keep pushing forward. He soon found a more receptive audience at the Louisiana Hayride, another country music venue, where his career began to take off.

Turning Rejection into Triumph

From there, Elvis continued to refine his style, blending country with rhythm and blues to create a sound that was uniquely his own. By 1956, he had released "Heartbreak Hotel," which became a number-one hit. His dynamic performances, charismatic persona, and groundbreaking music quickly captivated audiences, propelling him to unprecedented fame.[2]

Elvis's journey from rejection to becoming a cultural icon is a powerful example of perseverance. His story resonates not only with aspiring musicians but also with educators who face similar challenges in their professional lives.

My Personal Journey

Over the course of my career, I've applied for numerous education positions. In these hiring processes, I've frequently encountered the frustrating wall caused by technological systems set up by the districts.

Early on, I didn't really have any networking connections because I was in a new area of the state, and my friends and family were not connected in any way to the education field. I was alone, and didn't know anyone. I had to simply submit my applications blindly and hope for the best.

I would diligently turn in all the required paperwork—résumé, references, cover letter, certifications—and wait. The subsequent silence was often deafening. Rarely did I hear back, and I didn't know why.

Over time, I began to realize that my paperwork wasn't making it past the algorithms that sift through the countless applications. It was disheartening and, for many years, it felt like an invisible barrier stood between me and my future in education.

But in those moments of frustration, I eventually understood that the algorithms weren't a barrier, they were just an obstacle. I just had to learn how to get around them.

From there, each rejection pushed me to reevaluate how I presented myself on paper. I tried new ways to organize my résumé, sharpen my cover letters, and highlight my certifications in order to break through the filters. The process taught me inventiveness and the importance of iteration.

As I advanced in my career, I often had principals and superintendents ask me why I never applied to their districts. "Actually, I did!" I would reply. They were unaware that I had applied numerous times, only to be filtered out by systems designed to streamline the hiring process. It was a reminder of the importance of the human element that was missing in the initial stages of hiring—something no technological system could fully capture.

Now, as a leader, I recognize how many solid candidates are often passed over by systems designed to weed out unqualified applicants. I've made it a point with my team to review each person thoroughly, ensuring we don't miss out on someone who could bring exceptional talent and passion to our schools.

Lessons for Educators

Many educators, much like Elvis, encounter significant resistance when trying to pursue promotions or break into a new field. Administrators may be hesitant to give innovative teachers a shot, clinging instead to traditional approaches. This rejection can be discouraging, but it also presents an opportunity for educators to demonstrate resilience and creativity in overcoming obstacles.

1. **You gotta start somewhere.** Like Elvis as a truck driver, many educators start their careers in roles far away from where they want to be. But that's OK! Although working your way up the ladder can be tedious, it's often a necessary part of learning, growing, and becoming qualified for the job of your dreams.

2. **Seek alternative platforms**. When the Grand Ole Opry rejected him, Elvis found success at the Louisiana Hayride. Similarly, you can seek out other venues—be it different schools, districts, or educational conferences—where your ideas could be more warmly received.

3. **Believe in yourself.** You will undoubtedly face critique of your work. Some of it will be valid, but much of it won't. If you wouldn't seek advice from someone, don't listen to their criticism. Instead, have faith in yourself, and ask for input from those you trust.

4. **Be inventive.** Like the algorithms halting my applications, many things that appear to be roadblocks are merely speedbumps. Look for creative solutions to seemingly insurmountable challenges, and don't be afraid to make multiple attempts at getting what you

want.

Write Your Own Lyrics

1. Reflect on the jobs and positions you've had throughout your life. How did each one play a role in getting you to where you are today? How can the position you have now continue to propel you toward your dream job?

2. Have you ever had to take your talents elsewhere for them to be recognized and appreciated? If so, what did you learn about the type of environment you thrive in? If not, what about your current workplace allows you to be at your best?

3. How can you transform negative feedback or criticism into a source of motivation without allowing it to diminish your passion and purpose as an educator? In what ways will you use setbacks to strengthen your commitment to making a positive difference in the lives of your students?

---

1. Escott, Colin, "Elvis Presley," Country Music Hall of Fame, accessed December 11, 2024, https://www.countrymusichalloffame.org/hall-of-fame/elvis -presley/.

2. "Elvis Presley Biography," Graceland: The Home of Elvis Presley, accessed December 11, 2024, https://www.graceland.com/biography/.

CHAPTER 10

Breaking Down Barriers
The Supremes

I think music in itself is healing. It's an explosive expression of humanity. It's something we are all touched by. No matter what culture we're from, everyone loves music.

Billy Joel

In the vibrant but tumultuous backdrop of 1960s America, a group of young women from Detroit rose to prominence, forever changing the landscape of music and civil rights. The Supremes, composed of Diana Ross, Mary Wilson, and Florence Ballard, became one of the most successful Motown acts and one of the best selling girl groups of all time.

Their journey was not just about musical success; it was a powerful story of overcoming struggles, confronting societal barriers, and making significant contributions to the Civil Rights Movement.

The Birth of Icons

The Supremes were born out of the poverty-stricken Brewster-Douglass housing projects in Detroit. Initially formed as The Primettes in 1959, they were determined to break into the male-dominated music industry. After several lineup changes, they became The Supremes and signed with Motown Records in 1961.[1]

The Supremes faced numerous obstacles in their early years, including racial discrimination, limited opportunities, and internal conflicts. They were often relegated to secondary roles in the industry, and their initial recordings failed to make an impact. However, their breakthrough came with the release of "Where Did Our Love Go" in 1964, which became their first number-one hit.

The Civil Rights Movement and Internal Conflicts

The Supremes' rise to fame coincided with the Civil Rights Movement. As African American women, they became symbols of the movement, breaking racial barriers and challenging societal norms. Their success provided a powerful narrative of black excellence and contributed to the broader struggle for equality.

Their music also transcended racial and social boundaries, bringing people together regardless of their backgrounds. Hits like "Baby Love," "Stop! In the Name of Love," and "You Can't Hurry Love" became anthems that resonated with a diverse audience. In an era marked by segregation and racial tension, The Supremes' music served as a unifying force, showing the world that shared experiences could bridge divides.

Despite their success, The Supremes faced significant internal conflicts. The pressures of fame, personal differences, and management decisions led to tensions within the group. Florence Ballard's departure in 1967 and subsequent struggles highlighted the personal toll that their journey took on each member.

Legacy and Impact

The Supremes' legacy extends beyond their music. They broke down racial and gender barriers, paving the way for future artists.[2] Their success demonstrated the power of representation and the importance of dismantling stereotypes. They showed that with talent, determination, and unity, it is possible to overcome systemic obstacles and leave a lasting impact.

My Personal Journey

In my career, I've witnessed firsthand the profound injustices many of my colleagues have faced—falsehoods on social media, political attacks, relentless harassment during board meetings, and, in some instances, threats on their lives or against their families. In many cases, these attacks were rooted solely in the color of their skin or their willingness to challenge outdated norms.

These educators were some of the finest minds in public education. They led groundbreaking programs, pioneered essential reforms, and made real, measurable progress for all students. They were celebrated nationally, recognized in respected publications, and honored with awards.

Yet, for a small but loud minority, this progress was perceived as a threat to rigid ideologies and outdated belief systems. Despite their brilliance, the accolades, and the meaningful difference they made, these colleagues were treated as "not enough" or "too much" based on an agenda they could never satisfy.

The impact of this hatred is lasting and painful, sometimes pushing the best among us out of the field. However, these leaders, many of whom may never know how truly exceptional they were, inspired and ignited hope in other educators across the country.

In my experience, the education system desperately needs more of them, not fewer. If the world is to improve, we need these champions back—people whose courage, intelligence, and innovation drive progress forward for all our students. Their voices, resilience, diversity, and vision are what will carry us toward a more just, inclusive, and enlightened future.

Lessons for Educators

Educators play a crucial role in shaping the minds of future generations. By promoting inclusivity, advocating for equity, and challenging discriminatory practices within the education system, educators can contribute to social change, just like The Supremes did.

Here are a few ways to get started:

1. **Challenge societal barriers.** Educators, especially those from marginalized backgrounds, often face racial, gender, and other socioeconomic obstacles. Your role is not only to teach but also to advocate for and champion students from all backgrounds, challenging systemic inequities and promoting inclusion.

2. **Create impact beyond the classroom.** Just as The Supremes' music resonated across racial and social

divides, your influence doesn't have to be limited by the walls of your classroom. Look for opportunities beyond the school grounds to bring communities together, celebrate diversity, or connect with people of various backgrounds.

3. **Find strength in unity.** In education, internal conflicts can derail even the strongest initiatives. Whether it's navigating differing perspectives among colleagues or working through complex challenges, look for common ground; this is key to fostering a supportive and productive school environment.

4. **Use art as a bridge for understanding.** The Supremes used music to transcend social boundaries and reach people of all backgrounds. Similarly, you can use the arts as a powerful tool to foster understanding and unity among students. By integrating music, storytelling, painting, dance, and other forms of artistic expression, you can create a classroom environment where every voice feels valued.

Write Your Own Lyrics

1. Reflect on a time in your teaching career when you experienced or witnessed discrimination. How did you address it, and what lessons did you learn that can help you support colleagues or students in similar situations?

2. How do you promote inclusivity and equity in your classroom or school? What specific strategies or initiatives have been most effective in creating a more inclusive learning environment?

3. Think about a time when you faced internal conflicts

within your school or district. How did you navigate these conflicts, and what strategies did you use to find common ground and collaborate effectively with your colleagues?

---

1. "The Supremes: Timeless Classics That Defined an Era," CIO Women Magazine, accessed December 11, 2024, https://ciowomenmagazine.com/the-supremes-timeless-classics/.

2. Detroit Historical Society, "The Supremes," Encyclopedia of Detroit, accessed December 11, 2024, https://detroithistorical.org/learn/encyclopedia-of-detroit/supremes/.

CHAPTER 11

Challenging Expectations
Carole King

If everything was perfect, you would never learn and you would never grow.

Beyoncé

C arole King faced numerous rejections early in her career, largely because her style and ambitions were unconventional for the time. Although she was a talented songwriter, industry gatekeepers were hesitant to embrace her unique sound, which differed from the mainstream styles that record labels were seeking. Her lyrics and melodies were often deeper and more personal, which didn't align with the formulaic approach many artists and labels wanted during the 1960s.

From Songwriter to Performer

Additionally, King faced an uphill battle in establishing herself as a performer. The music industry was accustomed to seeing her behind the scenes as a songwriter rather than a front-and-center artist.[1] Critics were skeptical of her ability to make this transition, questioning whether her voice and presence were strong enough for the spotlight. Her path was complicated further by societal expectations around gender roles in music; female artists often encounter more scrutiny and pressure to conform to industry standards.

Despite these setbacks, King continued to refine her skills as a performer. She persevered through the criticism and rejection, maintaining a belief in her talent and potential. Her diligence paid off when she released her groundbreaking album, *Tapestry*, in 1971. The album was a massive success, earning four Grammy Awards and becoming one of the best selling albums of all time.[2]

My Personal Journey

There was a time earlier in my life when the people closest to me—family members and even some romantic partners—didn't fully believe that I was going to be successful. In their eyes, I wasn't capable of achieving something great, and they let me know it. In fact, someone even once wrote me a note telling me I would never amount to anything.

That note, those words, could have crushed me. They could have pushed me down a path of resentment, anger, and self-pity. But I refused to let them define my future. Instead of allowing those doubts to consume me, I used them as fuel. I realized that the only person who could determine my worth, my success, and my potential was me.

Every time I faced a challenge or a setback, I thought of those words—not with bitterness but with a quiet determination. They became fuel for the fire that pushed me forward when things got tough, driving me to work harder, to dig deeper, and to prove to them and myself that I could rise above the limitations others imposed on me.

Choosing self-control and resilience over resentment was not easy, but it was necessary. Kindling negativity would have only held me back. Instead, I turned that hurt into motivation, and I'm proud of the journey it continues to lead me on.

In the process, I've learned that success is less about proving people wrong and more about proving to yourself that you are capable of more than anyone imagined. You can transform doubts into stepping stones and use them to build the foundation of a life that's stronger and more resilient than you ever thought possible.

Lessons for Educators

Educational leaders frequently encounter unrealistic expectations from various quarters. Like Carole King, they may also find that others have put them in a box that limits their ability to grow and change. Whether it's parents questioning their decisions, community members skeptical of new initiatives, or colleagues resistant to change, challenging the status quo can be tough.

Below are some practical steps to help you to navigate these challenges:

1. **Highlight successful outcomes.** Just as King used *Tapestry* to demonstrate her talents and silence her critics, you too can focus on achieving measurable results. Demonstrating tangible improvements in students' learning outcomes can turn skeptics into supporters.

2. **Pursue lifelong learning.** King didn't become a performer by chance; she had to keep learning and growing in order to transform from a songwriter into an artist who owned the stage. Be hungry to keep learning, staying open to new ideas and approaches that allow you

to pivot and transform professionally.

3. **Be unique.** Your unique perspective and strengths are not to be constrained by others' expectations. Just as Carole King broke through industry norms, educators can leverage their individuality to challenge limitations and drive meaningful change in education.

4. **Remember your "why."** You once sat in an interview and told your potential employer that you were going to make a difference for each child in your classroom. Don't forget why you became an educator in the first place. That "why" will get you through many discouragements.

Write Your Own Lyrics

1. Reflect on a time you've silenced skeptics by delivering impressive results. How did that change the way others perceive you? How did it change the way you see yourself?

2. Consider your journey as a lifelong learner. How can you actively pursue new ideas, professional development, or strategies that allow you to evolve in your role, just as Carole King did in her transformation from songwriter to performer?

3. Remind yourself of the original passion and purpose that led you into education. Recall the goals and aspirations you had when you first started teaching. How can you reconnect with that initial drive and use it to stay motivated and focused on making a difference, especially when faced with resistance or setbacks?

1. Margolis, Lynne, "Carole King," Rock & Roll Hall of Fame, accessed December 11, 2024, https://rockhall.com/wp-content/uploads/2024/03/Carole_King_26746_RNRHF_2021_Highres-5.pdf.

2. "Carole King's Melody: A Brief History of the Legendary Musician," Broadway Rose Theatre Company, accessed December 11, 2024, https://www.broadwayrose.org/newsletter-summer2024/article3/.

CHAPTER 12

The Power of Passion
Taylor Swift

I believe musicians have a duty, a responsibility to
reach out, to share your love or pain with others.

James Taylor

In the heart of Reading, Pennsylvania, a young girl strummed her guitar, crafting songs that echoed her dreams and emotions. Taylor Swift, born in 1989, embarked on a journey that would take her from small-town talent shows to the pinnacle of global stardom. Her story is not just a tale of musical success but a beacon of inspiration.

Taylor Swift's early career was marked by an unwavering commitment to her passion. At just 11-years-old, she convinced her mom to take her to Nashville, the epicenter of country music, to pitch her songs to record labels. She and her mom walked down Music Row, handing out demos that were largely ignored. That didn't stop her, however. She continued to hone her craft, and at the age of 14, her family moved to Nashville to pursue her dream in earnest.

Once there, she pitched her songs to record labels only to face rejection after rejection, but she remained undeterred. Swift's perseverance paid off in 2005 when she became the youngest artist signed by the Sony/ATV Tree publishing house.[1]

Reinvention, Growth, and Resilience

Swift emerged as a country music star, and her transition from country music to pop nine years after her debut album was a bold move that demonstrated her ability to reinvent herself. With the release of her album, *1989*, in 2014, she embraced a new musical style that resonated with a broader audience. This shift not only expanded her fan base but also solidified her status as a versatile and innovative artist.[2]

Throughout her career, Taylor Swift has faced her share of criticism and setbacks. Public feuds, media scrutiny, and personal challenges could have derailed her. Instead, she used these experiences to fuel her creativity and artistic growth. Songs like "Shake It Off" and "Look What You Made Me Do" are testaments to her resilience and ability to turn adversity into strength.

Using Influence for Good

Beyond her music, Taylor Swift has used her platform to advocate for important causes. Whether it's championing women's rights, supporting education initiatives, or speaking out on social issues, Swift has demonstrated the power of influence and advocacy.

Swift's success is also a result of the support system she built around her. From her close-knit family to her loyal fans, Swift surrounds herself with people who believe in her vision and encourage her growth. Her collaborative spirit is evident in her numerous partnerships with other artists and her advocacy for musicians' rights.

My Personal Journey

When our school received the national SETDA Student Voice Award, the National Digital Principal of the Year award, and an invitation to the White House, it was an incredible honor, not just for me but for our entire school and community. I was able to attend with one of our dedicated teachers, and together, we celebrated the hard work and innovative spirit that brought us there. The community was overjoyed—seeing their school stand out and be recognized on such a prestigious platform brought a sense of pride and accomplishment.

You would think that everyone in the district, region, and state would have joined us in celebrating. But while we were embraced at home, the reception inside and beyond our district was far less enthusiastic. We had taken the limelight, and that did not sit well with everyone.

Coincidentally, just days after returning from Washington, we faced a surprise visit from the state fire marshal. What should have been a routine check-up quickly felt like something more. The marshal conducted a more thorough inspection than usual, scrutinizing some of the most innovative aspects of our school—the very things that had helped earn us national recognition.

Our hallways, which we had transformed into vibrant, interactive learning spaces with whiteboards and LEGO walls, were rigorously questioned. Our use of flexible seating and the fact that our middle-school students were among the first to use cellphones in the classroom were suddenly under investigation.

As the fire marshal walked through the building, I began to notice something strange. He used specific phrases that had only been brought up during a private board committee meeting—something no one outside of that room should have known.

While there was no way to be absolutely sure someone broke confidence, the coincidence was too glaring to ignore. It was evidence that our innovative approach to education had ruffled the feathers of the traditionalists. Those who preferred to keep education confined to rigid, outdated methods seemed determined to dim our light and reclaim attention.

That experience marked the first time I realized that innovation, while celebrated by some, can also spark resistance, especially when it shifts the status quo. I learned that not everyone welcomes change, particularly when egos and competition are involved. Some will go to great lengths to protect their own spotlight, even if it means undermining progress. Haters were gonna hate.

The experience taught me to be more mindful and more strategic. I realized that innovation is not just about having great ideas; it's about navigating the politics and resistance that come with bringing those ideas to life. Success in education requires not just vision but also the strength to stay the course, even when others try to dim your achievements.

By the way, the fire marshal finished that inspection with only one issue. He told the superintendent and me, "I wish my grandkids went to this school."

Lessons for Educators

Swift's career underscores the importance of passion and grit. Through her relentless pursuit of her dreams, her willingness to reinvent herself, and her ability to channel personal and professional setbacks into her artistry, Swift's journey offers invaluable lessons for those shaping the minds of future generations.

Here are some practical applications of these lessons:

1. **Pursue your passion relentlessly.** Most teachers didn't get into the education field for notoriety or financial wealth; they became educators because of a zeal for equipping future generations. Like Taylor Swift's unwavering dedication to her music since age 14, educators, too, need to approach their careers with commitment and a passion for education.

2. **Don't be afraid of reinvention.** Swift's shift from country to pop demonstrated her ability to reinvent herself to reach a broader audience. Similarly, educators must adapt to evolving educational landscapes, integrating new teaching methods, technologies, and standards. Regularly seek out professional development opportunities and stay informed about the latest educational trends in order to better meet the needs of your students and remain effective in your role.

3. **Protect your personal life.** Swift's personal life and relationships have influenced her music in authentic, meaningful ways, but they've also landed her in the spotlight of public scrutiny and criticism. Many educators also struggle with keeping their professional and personal lives separate, often bringing stress home with

them. It's important to find ways to leave the pressures of teaching at school so you can be fully present for your family, friends, and personal commitments.

4. **Be mindful of the forces working against change.** Swift's journey, like my own, is a reminder that success can attract admiration but may also bring resistance. Always be aware of the political, social, and personal forces influencing your school and district. No matter how successful your innovative ideas may be, these forces can undermine your efforts.

Write Your Own Lyrics

1. How can you leverage your passion for education to overcome the challenges in your day-to-day work as a teacher or administrator? How can this passion be a source of motivation when you feel discouraged or worn out?

2. In what ways do you struggle to protect your personal life from the pressures and difficulties at school? What strategies have you found helpful in maintaining work-life balance so you can be your best in the classroom and at home?

3. Think of a time when politics or social forces played a role in undermining an idea you had or an achievement you earned. What did you learn about navigating these tensions? Knowing what you know now, what would you do differently in a similar situation down the road?

1. "Life and Career," Taylor Swift
   Museum, accessed December 11, 2024,
   https://www.theswiftmuseum.com/life-and-career/.

2. Hudgins, Kristen, "How Taylor Swift Masterminded Global
   Success, Explained by SOMD Experts," University of Oregon
   School of Music and Dance, accessed December 11, 2024,
   https://musicanddance.uoregon.edu/TaylorSwift/.

CHAPTER 13

Overcoming Adversity
Andrea Bocelli

The best music is essentially there to provide you something to face the world with.

Bruce Springsteen

In the picturesque town of Lajatico, Italy, a young boy with a profound passion for music defied the odds. Andrea Bocelli, born in 1958, faced extraordinary challenges from the moment he came into the world. Born with congenital glaucoma, Bocelli was slowly losing his sight throughout his childhood. However, his family nurtured his love for music from an early age, recognizing his remarkable vocal talent and determination. His early years were not only defined by his visual impairment but also by an unyielding resolve to overcome the obstacles before him.

Despite his difficulties, Bocelli demonstrated a natural gift for music. His parents encouraged him to pursue his passions, and at the age of six, he began to play the piano, later adding the flute and the saxophone to his repertoire. Music, to him, became more than just an outlet for expression; it was a way to navigate the world when the world itself became harder to see.

A Life-Changing Moment

The greatest adversity of Bocelli's life came when he was 12 years old. While playing soccer, he was struck in the eye, which caused a traumatic injury. This event, combined with the progression of his glaucoma, resulted in total blindness.[1] For many, such a setback would have been crippling—physically and emotionally. Yet, for Bocelli, this tragedy sparked an inner strength that would define his future.

Rather than retreating into despair, Bocelli's blindness drove him to refine his musical talents in a new, deeper way. His desire to become a professional singer was now his lifeline. Though his path forward was filled with obstacles—both emotional and professional—he never allowed his blindness to become a barrier to his dreams. Instead, it became the catalyst for his resilience.

Battling Industry Skepticism and Personal Doubts

As Bocelli grew older, he faced skepticism not only from the world around him but also from within the music industry. Classical music, especially opera, has long been a field where conventional standards of appearance and performance are often prioritized. Bocelli's blindness made him a visible anomaly in a field that, historically, has been more focused on visual presence than on vocal prowess.

But Bocelli was undeterred. He studied law at the University of Pisa, but his heart remained with music. At night, he would sing in local bars and clubs to hone his craft. Despite his talents, breaking into the opera world was no easy feat. Early on, he faced rejection from prestigious conservatories, and many dismissed him as an "amateur" because of his lack of formal training. His dream seemed increasingly distant.

Yet, Bocelli's perseverance led him to a breakthrough. In 1992, a chance encounter with renowned Italian tenor Luciano Pavarotti changed his life.[2] Pavarotti, who had been moved by a recording of Bocelli's singing, invited him to sing a duet at a charity concert. This moment marked the beginning of Bocelli's international rise. However, even with this incredible opportunity, Bocelli had to overcome deep self-doubt and fear of being judged. His journey to global recognition was not immediate—it required years of hard work, auditions, and an unwavering belief in his craft.

Turning Adversity into Artistic Strength

Bocelli's blindness, rather than limiting him, has shaped his artistry in profound ways. His ability to connect deeply with music, unconstrained by visual distractions, allows him to convey emotion and passion in a way few artists can. In interviews, he has spoken about how music became his vision. His connection with every note and every lyric is often described as transcendent, as if he experiences music on a more intimate level than those who see.

Bocelli's performances are not merely technical feats—they are expressions of the soul. His voice, rich and emotive, carries the weight of his life experiences. Through his music, he communicates a message of hope, resilience, and the power of human connection, resonating deeply with audiences across the globe.

His 1995 album *Bocelli* marked a turning point in his career, reaching millions and opening doors to both classical and pop music audiences. Songs like *Con Te Partirò* (Time to Say Goodbye) became anthems of hope, speaking directly to the hearts of listeners who were also fighting their own battles. Bocelli's ability to transform pain into beauty has been one of the defining characteristics of his music.

My Personal Journey

For me, growing up with hearing loss wasn't just about the physical challenges—it was about battling the stigmas and stereotypes that came with wearing hearing aids. The assumption of adults in school was simple: A child who uses hearing aids should be in special education classes. So I refused to wear them, not because I didn't need them but because I didn't want to face the looks, the whispers, or the sense of being different.

Instead, I pushed through life working twice as hard as everyone else, learning to read lips, straining to hear, and constantly thinking about what was said before I could even begin to process it. This extra effort became my normal, though it often left me feeling exhausted and disconnected.

As I got older, people would tell me I had a unique accent. Some would say it was just the New Jersey in me, but others knew there was something more—something they couldn't quite pin down. That accent, though a reflection of my background and my hearing loss, was part of the identity I carried without fully understanding how deeply it was shaped by my silent struggles.

When I finally bought hearing aids, it was a decision rooted not only in necessity but in acceptance. I knew I needed them to do my job better as an educational leader, to ensure I could be fully present and effective in every conversation, meeting, and decision.

More importantly, I needed them in order to be the best father I could be—to hear my children clearly, to communicate with them in a way that ensured they didn't face the same speech struggles I did. I also wanted my daughter, who was also born hard of hearing, to have a role model, and someone who supported her daily. Once again, the looks and whispers started, but by that point, I had learned something important: What others thought of me was beyond my control, and it no longer mattered to me.

The journey of growing up with hearing loss taught me resilience, adaptability, and, ultimately, self-acceptance. I am thankful for who I am, for the challenges I've faced, and for the strength I've gained in overcoming them. My hearing loss no longer defines me, but it has certainly shaped the leader, the father, and the person I've become.

Lessons for Educators

Andrea Bocelli's journey from a young boy with a passion for music to a world-renowned tenor is a powerful reminder of the human spirit in the face of adversity. For educators, whether they have disabilities or not, his story serves as a beacon of inspiration, illustrating how challenges can be transformed into powerful sources of motivation and resilience.

Below are some things to try in your own school or classroom:

1. **Leverage disability as a unique strength.** For Bocelli, his vision loss is a superpower in many ways. It allows him to focus more on how his music sounds rather than on whatever visual stimuli might distract him. You can help students with disabilities discover their superpowers and

learn to use them in and out of the classroom.

2. **Inspire students to overcome their own challenges.**
   No doubt Bocelli has inspired hundreds of other blind
   musicians to pursue their dreams. When students see
   their teachers thriving despite significant challenges, it
   sends a powerful message: Obstacles do not define one's
   potential.

3. **Embrace creative and unconventional solutions.**
   Modifying the classroom to accommodate students
   with disabilities takes out-of-the-box thinking and a
   willingness to experiment. Be willing to devote extra
   energy to make the learning environment equitable for
   those who could fall behind otherwise.

4. **Maintain high expectations.** Despite common
   misconceptions, people with disabilities are often
   capable of living "normal" lives. You can allow for
   modifications and adjustments, but don't dumb down
   learning outcomes for students with physical, mental,
   emotional, or social limitations. Instead, give them the
   encouragement and accommodations they need to
   excel.

Write Your Own Lyrics

1. Reflect on your own disability or the disability of someone
   close to you. What is that disability's superpower? How
   does it benefit you or the person you know? How can you
   use this insight to help students with disabilities discover
   their superpowers?

2. What are some creative or experimental solutions you've
   tried out in the classroom to help a student with a

disability? Which ones have worked well and which ones haven't? How can you use what you've learned to inform the solutions you try in the future?

3. Think of a student with a disability who struggles with feeling different or "weird." Do you or other teachers, whether intentionally or inadvertently, lower learning expectations for this student? If so, what changes can you make so the student feels supported yet challenged?

---

1. "Is Andrea Bocelli blind? The story behind the famed tenor's sight loss," Classic FM, March 6, 2023, https://www.classicfm.com/artists/andrea-bocelli/blind-reason-sight-loss/.

2. "Andrea Bocelli," Biography.com, July 17, 2024, https://www.biography.com/musicians/andrea-bocelli/.

CHAPTER 14

Celebrating Differences
Wu-Tang Clan

Sometimes adversity creates an environment for good things to grow.

Rick Ruben

In the early 1990s, the streets of Staten Island, New York, bore witness to the genesis of a revolutionary force in hip-hop: the Wu-Tang Clan. Composed of nine members, each with unique personas and styles, Wu-Tang Clan redefined the rap game.[1] Their journey from obscurity to becoming one of the most influential groups in music history was fraught with challenges, internal conflicts, and the ever-present struggle for authenticity and success in the cutthroat music industry. For aspiring educators, their story provides a powerful analogy for overcoming obstacles and celebrating differences in the face of resistance.

The Birth of a Clan

The Wu-Tang Clan was officially formed in 1992, but its roots go back to friendships and collaborations that predated the group's creation. The core members—RZA, GZA, and Ol' Dirty Bastard—were cousins who had been involved in the music scene since the mid-1980s. They were later joined by Method

Man, Raekwon, Ghostface Killah, Inspectah Deck, U-God, Masta Killa, and lastly, Cappadona.

RZA, the group's de facto leader and primary producer, envisioned a collective where each member could pursue solo careers while still being part of the group. This unique approach allowed Wu-Tang Clan to operate both as a unified entity and a platform for individual success.

Grit and Authenticity

The Wu-Tang Clan's early days were marked by struggle and hardship. Many members faced criminal charges, legal troubles, poverty, and the consequences of urban decay. Their experiences shaped their music, giving it an edge and authenticity that resonated with listeners.

In 1993, they released their debut album, *Enter the Wu-Tang (36 Chambers)*, a raw and gritty masterpiece that showcased their unique hardcore hip-hop style. The album's success was not immediate, however; it grew gradually, fueled by the group's relentless promotion and the growing popularity of singles like "Protect Ya Neck" and "C.R.E.A.M."

Navigating Group Dynamics

As the group's popularity soared, internal conflicts began to surface.[2] The diverse personalities and ambitions of the members often led to tensions. RZA's vision and leadership style, while instrumental in their initial success, sometimes clashed with the desires of other members who wanted more creative control or different career paths.

Despite these conflicts, Wu-Tang Clan managed to stay together, largely due to their shared history and the loyalty they felt toward the collective.

Battling the Music Business

The Wu-Tang Clan's innovative business model, where each member was free to sign solo deals with different labels, was both a strength and a challenge. It allowed them to dominate the rap scene individually and collectively, but it also created complications with recording companies and contractual agreements.

Their unorthodox approach initially faced resistance from the music industry, which was not accustomed to such arrangements. Negotiating deals that benefited both the group and individual members required shrewd business acumen and perseverance.

The Wu-Tang Dynasty

Despite the myriad of challenges, the Wu-Tang Clan's impact on hip-hop is undeniable. Their second album, *Wu-Tang Forever* (1997), debuted at number one on the Billboard 200 and cemented their status as rap legends. Their influence extended beyond music, affecting fashion, language, and popular culture.

Each member also enjoyed varying degrees of solo success, with standout albums like Method Man's *Tical*, Raekwon's *Only Built 4 Cuban Linx...*, and Ghostface Killah's *Ironman* achieving critical and commercial acclaim. Their solo projects further solidified the group's legacy, proving the effectiveness of their collective and individual approach.

My Personal Journey

When I began coaching high school soccer, I came from a nationally ranked program where the players were greatly skilled, disciplined, and prepared for high expectations. In turn, I was used to systems that demanded precision, teamwork, and rigorous training.

However, when I took on a new team, I quickly realized that the players I was now coaching didn't have the same level of experience or training. My initial approach—implementing the techniques and strategies that had worked in my past—simply didn't resonate with them. The team struggled, and it was clear something had to change.

It was a humbling moment when I realized that success wouldn't come from trying to force the players into a mold they weren't ready for. I needed to adjust my approach and meet them where they were. Instead of focusing on what they couldn't do, I began to focus on what they could do.

We shifted to a system that emphasized their individual strengths and allowed each player to contribute in a way that matched their abilities. For example, the players came from diverse backgrounds, each bringing a unique style and perspective to the game. We turned that diversity into a strength, using it as a spark to ignite a sense of unity and purpose.

Slowly but surely, the players began to come together—not as individuals struggling to fit into a system but as a team that embraced their differences and used them to fuel success. With these adjustments, the team found its rhythm, and we went on to qualify for the state playoffs multiple times. Along the way, we built up a community feeder program, ensuring that the foundation we were laying would continue to grow for years to come.

Looking back, this experience taught me that leadership isn't about forcing people into preconceived notions of success—it's about adapting, listening, and finding ways to make everyone's strengths shine. The journey with that team was a powerful reminder of the value of adaptability, collaboration, and celebration of differences.

Lessons for Educators

Aspiring educators can draw inspiration from this model, understanding that collaboration and support within a team can amplify individual strengths and lead to greater success. However, keep in mind that working within a team of diverse educators with different ideas and methods can also lead to conflicts.

The story of Wu-Tang Clan is a helpful illustration of how embracing diversity can not only help teams resolve conflicts, but it can also foster resilience, collaboration, and collective success. Just as Wu-Tang members supported each other and pushed through industry resistance, educators can work together to bring innovative ideas to their schools, even when met with skepticism from administrators and boards of education.

Here are four practical action items for educators inspired by Wu-Tang Clan's story:

1. **Cultivate diverse skills and abilities**. Like Wu-Tang Clan, where each member brings unique styles and talents, educators should recognize and celebrate the diversity within their teams. Encourage your colleagues to share their individual strengths, and foster an

environment where different perspectives are valued. This approach not only enriches the learning experience for students but also creates a stronger, more cohesive team.

2. **Stay true to yourself.** Wu-Tang Clan's rise was marked by setbacks, but their authenticity kept them grounded and relatable. For an educator, staying true to who you are is crucial, especially when introducing innovative ideas that may face resistance. Stay committed to your vision and unique teaching style, and trust that your authenticity will resonate with both students and colleagues over time.

3. **Build collaborative frameworks.** RZA's vision allowed Wu-Tang members to pursue solo success while staying united as a group. Educators can apply a similar model by creating collaborative frameworks within their schools that support individual growth as well as a sense of community. Encourage cross-curricular projects, team-teaching initiatives, and mentorship opportunities to foster a supportive environment.

4. **Embrace adaptability in leadership.** Wu-Tang faced conflicts and challenges in group dynamics, but they persisted by adapting their approach. In education, flexible leadership styles that meet the needs of your team can lead to stronger relationships and improved outcomes. Instead of rigidly sticking to one way, try listening with openness to the needs and ideas of your colleagues.

Write Your Own Lyrics

1. In what ways can you leverage the diverse strengths

and perspectives of your colleagues to create a more inclusive, collaborative, and dynamic learning environment that fosters collective success as well as individual growth?

2. What does authenticity look like for you? What strategies can you use to stay true to yourself and your vision, particularly in the face of resistance from administrators or boards of education when introducing innovative ideas?

3. Reflect on a time when you had to adapt your leadership approach to meet your team members where they were. What adjustments did you make and how did those improve relationships and outcomes?

---

1. Garn, Talmage, "Wu-Tang Clan Members: A Comprehensive Guide," 92.5 the Beat, October 25, 2023, https://925thebeat.com/life/wu-tang-clan-members-a-com prensive-guide/.

2. Poisuo, Pauli, "The Troubled History of the Wu-Tang Clan," *Grunge*, September 24, 2019, https://www.grunge.com/167401/the-troubled-history-of-th e-wu-tang-clan/.

CHAPTER 15

The Alternative Route to Success
Toby Keith

Don't ever try and be like anybody else, and don't be afraid to take risks.

Waylon Jennings

B efore Toby Keith became a household name in country music, he had a life filled with hard work doing various blue-collar jobs. His journey from the oil fields of Oklahoma to the stages of Nashville offers a compelling narrative for those considering a career change.

The Oil Fields

Toby Keith Covel, born on July 8, 1961, in Clinton, Oklahoma, grew up with a strong work ethic instilled by his family. He spent his teenage years working at his grandmother's supper club where he was first exposed to live country music. This experience planted the seeds of his musical aspirations, but his journey to stardom was far from straightforward.

After high school, Keith took a job in the oil fields of Oklahoma.[1] The work was grueling and dangerous, involving long hours in harsh conditions. Despite the physical toll, Keith thrived in this environment, appreciating the camaraderie and sense of accomplishment that came with the job. He quickly moved up the ranks, becoming an operations manager.

Keith's time in the oil fields taught him the value of perseverance and resilience. These qualities would later prove invaluable in his music career.

Pursuing His Passion

While working in the oil fields, Keith never lost sight of his love for music. He formed a band called Easy Money, which performed at local bars and honky-tonks whenever possible. Balancing his demanding job with his musical pursuits was challenging, but Keith remained committed to his dream.

In 1982, the oil industry faced a severe downturn, leading to widespread layoffs. Keith found himself out of work, but instead of seeing it as a setback, he viewed it as an opportunity to focus on his music.

After moving to Nashville in the late 1980s, Keith faced significant rejection from major record labels. Despite his talent and ambition, he struggled to get noticed in a highly competitive industry. Keith was told that his music was "too raw" or "too country" for mainstream tastes, and he had difficulty securing a record deal. In an era when the country music industry was heavily dominated by polished, radio-friendly sounds, Keith's rougher, more authentic style didn't fit the mold. Keith took matters into his own hands.

In the early '90s, he recorded his first album, *Toby Keith*, on his own dime, believing in his ability to succeed. Without the backing of a major label, he struggled to get radio play and distribution, which made it difficult to gain traction. His persistence, however, led to a breakthrough when he began performing live shows and earning a fan base through his strong, relatable songs and down-to-earth personality.

Keith began playing gigs full-time, honing his skills and building a following. His big break came in 1993 when he released his debut single, "Should've Been a Cowboy," which topped the country charts and launched his career.[2]

My Personal Journey

I spent the first half of my life working on the back of a water well drilling rig where I experienced the true meaning of hard, manual labor. The long, grueling hours pushed my physical and mental limits.

I remember winter mornings where, already wet by 7 a.m., I'd stand next to the exhaust of a water pump just to stay warm while the temperature hovered around 34 degrees. Summers were equally unforgiving as I found myself shoveling under a relentless sun, never feeling cool enough.

When I decided to pursue a career in education, it was a world away from the one I had known. I had no family connections to this new field, and the shift was a mental adjustment in many ways.

I had to fit into a different culture and learn a new way of thinking about work ethic—one that wasn't measured by physical exhaustion but by intellectual engagement and emotional resilience. It required a different mindset, and I often struggled with self-doubt and uncertainty as I navigated this unfamiliar terrain.

The transition wasn't easy. I had to unlearn certain habits, like pushing through challenges with brute force, and instead adopt a more strategic, patient approach. At times, I questioned whether I had made the right choice, especially when the mental hurdles felt just as taxing as the physical ones I had left behind. But, in retrospect, those early experiences with hard labor taught me grit and determination, which I carried with me into this new chapter of life.

Lessons for Educators

For those considering a move to a different position within the education field, Keith's story serves as an inspiring reminder that it's never too late to pursue your dreams. By leveraging your existing skills, pursuing your passion, and staying committed to your goals, you can make a successful transition to another role in education where you have the opportunity to inspire and shape the minds of future generations.

Here are some steps to help you navigate the transition:

1. **Evaluate your skills and interests.** Reflect on your current job and identify the skills and experiences that are transferable to the job that you aspire to have. Consider what areas within education you are passionate about and why.

2. **Research educational requirements.** Investigate the certifications and educational requirements in your state or country that you'll need to achieve the career you're pursuing. You can start with an online search, but for more detailed information, you may need to reach out to the agencies responsible for education in your area.

3. **Gain experience.** Look for opportunities to gain

experience working in your desired field through mentorships, administrative office duties, and/or interning in a department that you are interested in. Hands-on experience can provide valuable insights and help you build your résumé.

Write Your Own Lyrics

1. What skills and experiences from your current job can help lay a solid foundation for advancing your career? How can you leverage those to enhance your effectiveness in your new role and bring unique perspectives to the classroom, school, and/or district?

2. What are the requirements for your dream job? What certifications, credentials, or other qualifications will you need to obtain? Begin making a plan for how you'll meet these requirements and gain the experience you'll need.

3. Considering the adaptability and resilience Keith demonstrated in transitioning from the oil fields to a music career, how can you prepare yourself to embrace and navigate the uncertainties and changes that will come with your career shift?

---

1. Oklahoma Historical Society, "Keith, Toby (1961–2024)," *The Encyclopedia of Oklahoma History and Culture*, accessed December 9, 2024, https://www.okhistory.org/publications/enc/entry?entry=KE016/.

2. KBOE Radio, "Toby Keith on the Deadline That Almost Stopped His Career," December 26, 2018, https://kboeradio.com/toby-keith-on-the-deadline-that-almost-stopped-his-career/.

Conclusion

You build on failure. Use it as a stepping stone and close the door on the past. Don't try to forget the mistakes, but don't dwell on it.

Johnny Cash

As this musical set list draws to a close, it's essential to reflect on the powerful lessons we've uncovered together—lessons for educators who dare to innovate, challenge the status quo, and persevere in the face of rejection. This book is more than a collection of stories from iconic musicians; it's a manifesto for resilience, courage, and growth.

In *Grit: The Power of Passion and Perseverance,*[1] researcher Angela Duckworth highlights how setbacks—rather than deterring the most successful individuals—often drive them to refine their approach and their goals. Her work demonstrates that what drives achievement is not genius, talent, or luck, but a formidable combination of zeal and tenacity in the face of resistance.

Every educator, regardless of their title, will face rejection at some point in their career—whether it's a failed proposal, a denied promotion, an overlooked idea, or an undervalued initiative. But what if, like Tom Petty, we saw every no as a necessary push toward a greater yes? What if, like Johnny Cash, we viewed hardship as the crucible that forges strength?

The artists profiled in this book were not immune to failure. They were tested by it, beaten down by it, defined by it, and ultimately strengthened by it. Their stories remind us that greatness is often born from adversity, and that rejection is simply a redirection toward something better.

As educators, the parallels to our daily challenges are unmistakable. The classrooms we lead, the students we inspire, and the colleagues we collaborate with all present unique trials. But as we've seen through the lens of musical legends, rejection is never the end; it is often the beginning of something transformative. A closed door is an opportunity to rethink our approach, adapt, or innovate in ways we never would have imagined.

This book's call to action is clear: Turn rejection into fuel for growth. But it doesn't stop there. It urges you to reflect deeply on your own practice, your own story. Let's take a look back at the main takeaways:

Resilience Overcomes Rejection

The most consistent theme throughout this book is the power of resilience. The Allman Brothers Band struggled for years before their sound was finally embraced. They never gave up.

For educators, this is a critical lesson. Rejection from colleagues, administrators, parents, or even students is not a reflection of your value or potential—it's a challenge to persevere and refine your approach and/or change your environment. When faced with obstacles, draw on your inner reserves and move forward with greater strength.

Find Your True Allies

The stories of George Harrison stepping in to support Tom Petty or Dr. Dre mentoring Eazy-E emphasize the importance of having advocates who believe in you. In education, find those allies who will help carry your ideas forward when others can't see their potential. Surround yourself with those who recognize your vision and will champion your efforts even when others doubt you.

Reflect, Refine, Rebound

Every chapter of this book offers examples of self-reflection leading to breakthroughs. Johnny Cash's road was not easy, but it was his authenticity—his willingness to face personal and professional demons head-on—that made him a legend.

Educators, too, must continuously reflect on their practice, not just when things are going well, but especially in moments of doubt and struggle. Rejection is an opportunity to refine your approach, to recalibrate, and to emerge stronger.

Innovation Thrives on Risk

Miles Davis never stopped evolving, and neither should you. His relentless pursuit of new sounds, new approaches, and new collaborators reflects the spirit of true innovation, which leads to something better each time. Things that made you successful in the past won't always make you successful in the future.

In your role as an educator, don't shy away from risks. Implement bold strategies, introduce innovative methods, and challenge the educational norms. If something doesn't work, it's not failure—it's a stepping stone to success.

Perseverance Shapes Legacy

The long-term impact of the individuals profiled here was not built on immediate success. Bob Dylan didn't become an icon overnight. His journey, filled with criticism and rejection, was a testament to the power of perseverance.

Although members of Wu-Tang Clan each grew up in tough situations (some even went to jail), they never gave up on their dreams. Toby Keith could have stayed in the oil field, as he put in the hours to rise up in the ranks. However, when adversity hit, he took a chance on himself by recording his first album with his own money and achieved superstardom because of that.

As an educator, your legacy will not be shaped by a single year, a single project, or even a single student. It will be the culmination of your perseverance through each rejection and every challenge, and your unwavering commitment to the craft of teaching and the world of education.

Now, it's your turn to rise up and take to the stage. What will you do differently? How will you take these lessons of resilience, innovation, and perseverance into your own practice? Let this book serve as a catalyst for action.

As you saw at the end of each chapter, your story is still being written. Write your own lyrics. How you choose to respond to rejection, how you grow from failure, and how you persist in the face of adversity will define your legacy. Reflect deeply, act boldly, and remember that rejection is never the end of the song—it is the beginning of a new, more meaningful verse!

So stand your ground. Face setbacks with a new mindset. Embrace rejection as redirection. And like those who came before you—don't back down.

---

1. Duckworth, Angela, 2018, *Grit: The Power of Passion and Perseverance,* Scribner.

I Won't Back Down Playlist

R eading about legendary musicians and their tales of triumph is powerful, but *hearing* the fruits of their labor makes it all real.

I've put together a playlist of some of my favorite songs from the musicians discussed in this book as well as other artists whose resilience in the face of rejection is a source of inspiration for me. I hope you enjoy listening!

To access my playlist, please scan the QR code below.

About the Author

Glenn Robbins has served as a school superintendent in New Jersey since 2016. Prior to becoming a superintendent, he was a middle school principal, a high school assistant principal, a high school social studies teacher, and a high school varsity coach. He has been recognized across the globe for his innovative school and district improvement methods, and has been featured in numerous conferences, books, podcasts, and other publications.

Glenn has been named a Top 100 Educational Influencer in the U.S., NASS Technology (AI) Innovation and Application Superintendent of the Year, NASSP Digital Principal of the Year, a National Superintendent of the Year finalist, and a EDTECH Digest International District Leadership finalist. He has received numerous international, national, and state recognitions, including the National Exemplar of Education award, the Northeast Innovative Superintendent award, the NJ Visionary Superintendent award, the Samsung Solve for Tomorrow award, and the SETDA Student Voice award.

Glenn is also the proud recipient of a National Superintendent Certification and is co-chair of the NJASA Technology Committee. He serves as an AASA National Governing Board member, Digital Promise League of Innovative Schools member, and an AASA Aspiring Superintendent mentor. He is also a bestselling author of *Calm in the Chaos: Ancient Stoic Wisdom for Successful School Leadership*.

If you'd like Glenn to come speak to your team, facilitate a workshop, coach you individually, or provide mentorship at scale, contact him at https://glennrobbins.com.

www.ingramcontent.com/pod-product-compliance
Lightning Source LLC
Chambersburg PA
CBHW061652120626
46550CB00003B/920